ATHEISM
VERSUS
BELIEF

Arguments For and Against Religion

Crescent Books

International Acclaim for
Atheism Versus Belief

"Accessible, insightful, and patient … Brandon Mayfield does not evade the tough questions; in fact he does a great job at addressing them head on, in a manner that most can relate to and understand."

—***Crescent Reviews***

"This book deals with a topic which is playing a very important role and will be playing a much bigger role in the future. Seeing that both atheism and agnosticism are on the rise, this work is extremely important!"

—**Stef Keris**, author of *Europe's Forgotten Ottoman Heritage* and founder of Al-Muqaddima

"A lucid and thoughtful book … well written and researched. This is a book for anyone who aspires to understand past and current atheism versus belief arguments and the debates."

Burhan al-Din Fili, author of *The Spectacular Escape*

"In an age of increasing secularism and rejection of faith, Brandon Mayfield's book evenly presents a clear view of both sides —disbelief and belief in God— while profoundly and intelligently addressing and responding to the toughest arguments often made in support of atheism. His book stands out as a timely and much needed work that serves to eradicate the false perceptions around belief in God."

—**Marwa Assar**, author of *The Compass HOME*

"Brandon Mayfield's *Atheism Versus Belief* stands out for its unique, reflective, straightforward, and well-reasoned approach, working to rectify the misconceptions about religious belief often propagated by certain modern atheists. While unpacking these new trends, the book also delves into the significant impact global faiths like Islam have made on society at large, especially when it comes to shaping our thinking and understanding of the Creator and His creation."

—**Flamur Vehapi**, author of *Ertugrul Ghazi: A Very Short Biography*

"This is definitely an essential and recommended read for the academic and the neophyte, the curious and the person in a hurry."

—**Naser Bresa**, professor, and author of *Retrospektiva*

ATHEISM
VERSUS
BELIEF

Arguments For and Against Religion

Brandon Mayfield
co-author of *Improbable Cause*

Crescent Books

Crescent Books

First Published in November 2023
by Crescent Books
an imprint of Crescent Institute LLC
Portland, OR.
e-mail: crescent.books2020@gmail.com

Prepared and Typeset
by Erzen Pashaj

Paperback
ISBN: 978-1-954935-04-4
Subjects:
Religion | Faith | Philosophy
Atheism | Debates
Islam

First edition
Includes bibliographical references.
Text copy edited by Stella Williams
and Caitlin Dwyer
Cover image: ESA/Hubble & NASA
Cover design: Elipse Productions

Printed in the United States of America

Dedication

To Mona, Shane, Sharia, Samir and Sumaya,
for whom I hold so dear.
To the rest of my family and friends
for their love, patience, wisdom,
and understanding.
And to all of them who have
made my life fuller,
including those one step ahead
of us but no longer with us.

CONTENTS

PART I: ARGUMENTS FOR AND AGAINST GOD: ATHEISM, SCIENCE, AND RELIGION

PART II: RELIGION: ORIGINS, AUTHENTICITY AND BASIC BELIEFS

INTRODUCTION

Belief in God, or not, is the most overarching filter for our perceptions, personal interactions, social institutions, morality, and general cosmology. Most atheists argue that organized religion only causes strife and bloodshed, holding us as prisoners, keeping us from evolving individually and as a community due to outdated myths and superstitions.[1] Science, they argue, disproves religion and is the only way forward. Those who believe in God tell us that an omnipotent Creator has a divine plan that rewards or punishes us for our actions, even in some instances to include eternal bliss or perpetual hell.[2] The stakes could not be any higher. Belief in God may be holding back all of humanity or it may be humanity's only salvation, and yet we give little serious effort in establishing the strength or weakness of either camp's tenets or arguments.

Faith in God or skepticism in such belief has been around since the dawn of history. Cycles of religious fanaticism followed by secular skepticism are all too common. Even on a personal level, we vary from time to time in the character and intensity of our beliefs or disbelief. In light of modern advancements in science and the widespread acceptance of the theory of evolution, belief in God has been re-examined and re-evaluated. In this process of re-evaluation, many have abandoned the notion of God as a viable theory altogether.

And yet today, there is still a steady march of proselytizers from both atheists and believers, religious missionaries and secular mouthpieces, ever eager to spread the message or call to arms.

Sometimes the calls to arms are real and not ideological.[3] Belief veils our political affiliations, often aligning religious conservatives of the-spare the rod-spoil the child ideology against so-called corrupt liberal seculars. More often, though, in politics and institutionalized religion such religious demarcations and rhetoric are merely tools for party establishment objectives and their secular economic interests.

On a personal level we are warned not to discuss religion and politics at work or with strangers because of the potential for strife, disagreement and discord that it can cause. But why such a potential for strong discord? Shouldn't we want to hear what the other is saying, carefully evaluate it, and then share with intellectual sincerity our own beliefs and prejudices in the hope of changing their mind or our own? In theory, that sounds preferable but in reality, why does this rarely happen? Is it because we have such deeply entrenched beliefs? Or is it because of the cognitive dissonance experienced when confronted with new information that conflicts with our existing affiliations, values and ideas?

Religions like beliefs come in many varieties, and often their tenets are clearly incompatible with one another. However, there are common elements shared by all of the world's great religions.[4] The purpose they provide varies depending on the time, location, and peoples. For different cultures, past and present, the role religion plays as an explanation for why things are and how they came to be is not that different from the role science plays for us in Western society today. One important reason that science and religion currently appear to be at odds is the perception that religion (primarily Judeo-Christian) is incompatible with evolution. While it is true that Christianity, if taken literally, has been construed to be contrary to modern theories of evolution, it is not true that believers have never entertained the notion of evolution. Nor is it true that such a notion of evolution did not pre-date Darwin, as most modern atheists suppose.

Some assert that Darwin's theory of evolution disproves the Bible and, more importantly, challenges the teleological argument (divine purposive explanation for existence) by allowing natural selection as an alternative to intelligent design. By demonstrating a means by which basic unintelligent forces can incrementally develop ever more complex structures, some suggest that an intelligent Designer is not necessary to explain the complexity and diversity we see in nature. But Darwin's theory has been used to presume more than it intended to show.[5]

While it is true that such complexity may come about by simple, seemingly unintelligent forces, for them to come about in such a functional, cohesive, and apparently purposeful way may lend itself to an argument for intelligent design just as (or more) easily as random design. Moreover, the balance and interrelationship between systems, objects, and various substances at every level imaginable (with a current caveat for the quantum level) is a strong indicator of at least inherent purpose and structure in nature, if not the product of intelligent design. On the flip side, the advocates of irreducible complexity want to show that certain biological features cannot be purely the product of Darwinian evolution. These demonstrations are likely to prove fruitless, but in so failing they will not end the God-or-not debate.

Instead, where there is evidence that religion (particularly Islam) may support not only biological evolution but a much more comprehensive, all-pervasive evolution (including abiogenesis and cosmological evolution), it becomes somewhat easier to reconcile with science. Both science and religion have always been readily disposed to being looked at under the umbrella of philosophy. They are not incompatible, overlapping magisteria, residing in completely different realms as our modern atheists proclaim.

Modern physics tells us that waves and oscillating fields are the predominant forces present throughout nature. They are the means by which information can be sent and received. Studies in quantum mechanics (of subatomic particles and energy) and neurology are starting to show us ways in which consciousness may be preserved, maintaining connections across both space and time (and perhaps even after death). Although science and religion once appeared to be diverging, we are beginning to find they are coming together in some respects.

The more we learn in science and physics the more we begin to understand that the basement of reality is information or something akin to consciousness or intelligence. For information to have meaning, it has to exist in syntax, that is rules for its various arrangements. And if language is a means by which information is communicated and conveyed, then it is becoming increasingly apparent that consciousness is the means by which reality is communicated and conveyed. In other words, nature exists to give consciousness self-expression.

The Bible, as well as the Quran, describe the word of God not only as scripture but also the means by which God's will is manifested into reality. When coupled with Eastern cosmologies such as Taoism, Hinduism, and Buddhism, we get the sense of a unified intelligence or consciousness somehow ever-permeating and sustaining the entire universe and all comprehensive reality. Some of the earliest Greek philosophers had a similar understanding in mind.[6]

We commonly see over time that religion tends to become trivialized and disregarded when simplistic, literal, even anthropomorphic explanations are given for God's characteristics and dominion over reality and the cosmos. Yet the cosmological transitions described in the Quran and Genesis in the Bible, when seen in terms of epochs, are surprisingly consistent with our current understanding of the physics of the origins and development of the cosmos.

Many of the attacks leveled against religion are based on texts that, by most modern scholarship, are not authentic or in some cases self-admittedly commentary. These texts naturally are subject to change or alteration when they are recorded decades, even centuries, after the events they supposedly describe. But, because there are independent sources and evidence that many if not all of the stories they describe have an historical basis, they should not be altogether discarded or summarily dismissed. On the other hand, a growing majority of modern physicists and cosmologists believe that religion is an outdated mode of explaining our place in the universe and objective views of reality. Take, for example, Caltech physics professor Sean Carroll.

In his lectures and debates, Carroll argues that God is not a good theory and there is no life after death and no physical means for consciousness to survive death. He admits that he has no trouble believing if God exists then life should exist. He estimates that the God theorists' best argument would be the fine tuning of physical parameters in our universe such as energy density, universe expansion, mass of electrons, and boundary conditions in the early universe. He accepts that these parameters are not what you expect as natural or necessarily random, and thus understands how one might wonder whether it is a product of intelligent design. Carroll's explanation for this fine tuning is that either we just got lucky, life is a lot more generic than we think, the selection effect within a multiverse, or admittedly design.[7]

Carroll is leaning strongly toward the selection effect within a multiverse. In other words, in an infinite universe, or number of universes, he can imagine regions of all different kinds of parameters and we just happen to be in that portion that is hospitable to life. He understands that theists can say that for every physical mechanism at play in the universe, it's simply because God made it that way. But that's a story he can tell without invoking God at all. He does some reverse engineering and asks if God existed, why make a universe with a hundred billion other galaxies when we only need one. Why do we have evil, random suffering, and more importantly what he describes as the problem of instruction? If the universe was created by a caring, omnipotent God, the first thing he would expect is God to explain himself. The Caltech professor says it would be very easy for God to give us some clues, such as "matter is made of atoms, the universe is billions of years old, people of different races and sexes and genders and sexual orientations should be treated equally, governments should derive their power from the consent of the governed," etc.[8]

There are two potential problems with this line of thinking. First, if you believe – as most modern scientists do – that people and our understanding of the world has evolved, then it would not have made sense to reveal natural explanations that would have been way ahead of their time. Imagine telling a cave-dwelling human in pictograph that atoms make up matter, or that the universe was billions of winters and summers old, for example. Instead there is a theme running through the Judeo-Christian-Islamic religion that finds God's message or instructions being revealed at specific times suitable for its followers. Second, it is presuming in some value-laden way that our modern prescriptions for the way things are or ought to be are right. One could agree that equal treatment and responsible governments could be beneficial for the masses in some estimation. But one could just as easily disagree and follow a contrary belief, such as he with the biggest stick can do and take whatever he wants. In other words, we would be substituting our own relatively impotent, subjective judgment for what we think an omnipotent being would or should do for what an omnipotent being has done or would necessarily do.

Religious texts such as the Torah, the New Testament, and the Quran are not first and foremost science books, nor do they profess to be. But they do profess to be instruction books of sorts, as Carroll predicts, assuming they were God-given. And yes, in some instances they do instruct more than just how to live our lives. And when that happens sometimes the proclamations about the physical universe based on religious texts are clearly wrong. When these proclamations are incompatible with our current objective understanding of nature, their adherents sometimes claim conveniently that they are only figurative. Occasionally, though, the natural proclamations ring accurate and sometimes what were once held to be figurative interpretations, with the advent of scientific discovery, appear literal.

Society can benefit from concepts that try to harmonize science and religion, knowing that any attempt is only an approximation and not an absolute; it is an effort for better and more useful understanding, knowing that ultimately these concepts are only transitory and not permanent. To not know it all, though, does not mean that it is not all objectively real. Science is a method of trying to verify the best we can the correlation between what is real and what we perceive. That species of modern science seems to have taken an unnecessary trend toward agnosticism or atheism. But science and religion or belief in a supreme being or a universal intelligence, are not, and should not be, considered antagonistic to one another.

Popular science commentator and astrophysicist Neil deGrasse Tyson says that if you use God for the explanation of every unknown phenomenon but through empirical investigations you find answers to these once unknowns, "then God is an ever-receding pocket of scientific ignorance."[9] Tyson himself believes God and science are incompatible and any attempt to reconcile them are likely to be unfruitful. He even posits that religion can, under the right conditions, hold people from advancing in their understanding, using Islam as an example. With some 2 billion

Muslims in the world today, he wonders why since 1900 only two Muslims have won the Nobel Prize whereas Jews, being much less populous, have won 80 times more Nobel prizes. Tyson attributes this rather simplistically, as other orientalists have, to Imam Al Ghazali, a 12th century Islamic scholar, for discouraging science and mathematics whereas up to his time, as Tyson admits, Baghdad was the intellectual capital of the world. Although too over-reaching in his explanation for this intellectual decline, his point is well taken.[10]

Al Ghazali did discourage certain philosophical inquiry which he considered as largely *kalam* (empty talk), but he also achieved an impressive assimilation of Islamic thought, practice, and jurisprudence and helped develop more consensus between Sunni (traditional) and Sufi (spiritual) practitioners, among many other achievements.[11] Al Ghazali was not opposed to mathematical sciences but rather to some of the leading scientific scholars of his day (such as Ibn Sina and Al Farabi) who proposed ideas at odds with Islam not supported by science or mathematics. In fact, he warned against denying objective science stating, "Great indeed is the crime against religion committed by anyone who supposes that Islam is to be championed by the denial of these mathematical sciences. For the revealed Law nowhere undertakes to deny or affirm these sciences, and the latter nowhere address themselves to religious matters."[12]

Al Ghazali's writings and attacks undoubtedly did have some impact in quelling a growing atmosphere of inquiry even if it was not his primary objective. That being said, Islam, as a rational and comprehensive religion, provided a solid foundation of objective inquiry, a point which cannot be overemphasized. Virtually every modern advancement in science, astronomy, medicine, and mathematics, can trace in part its roots to Muslim origins.[13] One can also confidently argue that Judaism, Christianity, and Islam provided society a stability and foundation that allowed science and culture to develop – and yet today there is an apparent gap between Science and Religion, Belief and Skepticism, East and West. But is that gap real or merely a mirage? Let us explore more together.

Brandon Mayfield
Oregon, 2023

PART I

ARGUMENTS FOR AND AGAINST GOD: ATHEISM, SCIENCE, AND RELIGION

-A-

A SUMMARY OF ARGUMENTS AND DEBATES

1

Popular arguments for the existence of God

"A little philosophy inclineth man's mind to atheism, but depth in philosophy bringeth men's minds about to religion."

~ Francis Bacon, Essays: Of Atheism, 1625

There are three popular arguments for the existence of God: teleological, ontological, and moral. The ontological argument deals with the very source of being itself. Proposed by St. Anselm and expanded upon by Descartes, it presupposes that God is "that [being] which nothing greater can be conceived," and thus it is obvious and knowable independent of any experience other than learning the language in which the concept – in this case, God – is expressed. But just because you can conceive it does not necessarily make it true. It is therefore the least compelling of the three arguments.

More popular and enduring is the teleological argument: that final causes, design, and purpose exist in nature. Today it is more commonly discussed in terms of intelligent design. This argument was evident in the writings of the early Greek philosophers known as the stoics who believed in a deep-rooted natural order or cosmic determinism. They believed that virtue and tranquility arose from balancing cosmic determinism with free will in an effort to maintain a will that is in accord with, and not at odds with, nature. Similarly, Aristotle accepted a cosmic intelligence to be responsible for this natural order but rejected a larger Maker and Sustainer entity. Instead he favored a non-creationist approach.

St. Thomas Aquinas, the 13th century Christian philosopher and theologian, presented the teleological argument as one of five ways in which he attempted to prove the existence of God. Because the "things which lack knowledge," such as rocks and planets, cannot cognizantly decide their own way in the universe, "[t]herefore some intelligent being exists by whom all natural things are directed to their end."[14]

The much-celebrated 17th century English physicist and mathematician Sir Isaac Newton, who formulated much of our modern natural physics, also ascribed strongly to this form of proof or argument. In his *Principia*, he wrote, "This most elegant system of the sun, planets, and comets could not have arisen without the design and dominion of an intelligent and powerful being."[15] And later when writing to a friend remarked, "When I wrote my treatise about our Systeme I had an eye upon such Principles as might work with considering men for the [belief] of a Deity, and nothing can rejoice me more than to find it useful for that purpose."[16]

The German philosopher Gottfried Wilhelm Leibniz, like Aristotle, did not disagree with an intelligent designer, only that the designer was not frequently intervening to keep nature moving. He proposed instead a metaphysics of simple substance in which the synchronicity of all substance could only have a predetermined source, as in a creator.

Leibniz, a contemporary of Newton, wrote:

> According to [Newton's] doctrine, God Almighty wants [i.e. needs] to wind up his watch from time to time; otherwise it would cease to move. He had not, it seems, sufficient foresight to make it a perpetual motion.[17]

The watch analogy was used most effectively by 18th century English Christian philosopher and utilitarian William Paley:

> Let's say you're walking around and you find a watch on the ground. As you examine it, you marvel at the intricately complex interweaving of its parts, a means to an end. Surely you wouldn't think this marvel would have come about by itself. The watch must have a maker. Just as the watch has such complex means to an end, so does nature to a much greater extent. Just look at the complexity of the human eye. Thus, we must conclude that nature has a maker too![18]

But modern atheists dismiss such design, arguing instead that by successive incremental steps, you can form something intelligible without the need for intelligence. Even Darwin admitted that if a complex organ – such as the eye, for example – "existed which could not possibly have been formed by numerous, successive, slight modifications," his theory would fail.[19]

Thus, the current most popular argument against God appears to be reducible complexity, while the best for God is irreducible complexity. The problem with these arguments is both camps can be right and wrong. For example, it is possible to conceive of God designing nature and the universe with cause and effect and incremental change sufficient enough to produce, over time, complex structures. In this sense God can be the source of all nature and its inherent characteristics even if it may display reducible complexities. On the other hand, it is possible to show that certain structures are irreducibly complex and an explanation other than natural selection can be offered. But natural selection is not necessarily antithetical to intelligent design or even creationism.

To be sure many mainstream proponents of creationism (a narrower theistic intelligent design theory) reject natural selection, based heavily on religious tenets and interpretations. For instance, the belief that the earth is less than 10,000 years old stems from a compilation of Biblical genealogies from the beginning of humanity to present. The archbishop of the church of Ireland, James Ushher, was one of the first to officially compile these genealogies in 1650 when he published his annals of the world showing the earth to have been created in 4004 BCE. By this dating the slow incremental crawl of natural selection would be impossible by all currently known biological models to produce the variety and complexity of organisms we see today, and would even deny the existence of dinosaurs. This is, of course, problematic.

Kant, an 18th century contemporary of Paley, rejected both the ontological and teleological arguments because he believed, like the British empiricists before him, that reason is too limited to know anything beyond human experience. As to the ontological argument, that the concept of God is self-evident, he said, "existence is not a predicate" (to merely say something exists does not add to the essence of a thing). Because we can have no knowledge of anything outside of experience or space and time, we cannot have certainty of God. Instead Kant believed that God's existence was a moral imperative and God's existence is necessary if we are to have any objective moral standards. Although he presupposed it, he did not provide a very convincing proof of it. Instead he offers what he describes as the highest good and suggests that a rational moral being must will the highest good. How does one know God or such higher good? According to Kant, primarily through intuition of his duty which is a dictate to pure reason.

Although Kant is highly regarded as one of the most influential philosophers in modern western philosophy, he is not without his detractors. Ayn Rand, a popular 20th century philosopher and novelist, is notorious for her attacks on Kant, even blaming him, unfairly, for bringing back religious mysticism. Firmly grounded in her atheistic worldview, she rejected the notion of a divine entity or higher power shaping human existence. For Rand, the concept of God was incompatible with her philosophy of Objectivism, which emphasized reason, individualism, and personal responsibility. She argued that the belief in God undermines human autonomy and rationality, positioning humans as subservient to an unknowable and arbitrary supernatural power.

Rand, instead of relying on some squishy-feely sense of moral imperative or reality, asks us to rely on our own mind with confidence and certainty and pride. Man is provided, she says, with a "sense of life" or "an emotional, subconsciously integrated appraisal of man and of existence … Every choice and value-judgment implies some estimate of himself and the world around him …" To the extent we are mentally active and focused in our thoughts, our sense of life is a brilliant product of a "rational philosophy." However, when we are passive in our mental faculties, our sense of life is shaped by random chance influences, impressions, associations and "snatches of environmental bromides by cultural osmosis."[20]

Rand despises Kant for his subordination of reason and certainty and for his selfless moral imperative, but more than this: for his belief in God based on nothing more than feelings or emotions and intuitions. She substitutes our own rational judgment for the judgment of an unknown, unseen, omnipotent God. Rand is afraid of centuries of subconscious philosophy acting on the subconscious mind of weak individuals. Such an individual "finds himself living with a sense of unknown, undefinable doom, as if in expectation of some approaching judgment day. What he does not know is that every day of his life is judgment day – the day of paying for the defaults, the lies, the contradictions, the blank-outs recorded by his subconscious on the scrolls of his sense of life."[21]

We find in the writings of Kant and Rand the age-old and current quandary of what guides our moral compass. If God, how do we know what that higher good is, and if not, why not whatever we choose?

Rand understood that "[a] philosophic system is an integrated view of existence," and we all have one.[22] In her estimation you define your philosophy by logical deliberation or by an accumulation of subconscious garbage of "unidentified wishes, doubts and fears, thrown together by chance."[23] Or, in her words, a "mongrel philosophy ... like a ball and chain in the place where your mind's wings should have grown."[24]

Rand continuously emphasizes how important it is to organize, train, and focus one's sense of life and to be aware of the myriad of ideas competing for your mind. For Rand knows all too well who "sets the tone of a culture ... a small handful of men: the philosophers. Others follow their lead, either by conviction or by default."[25]

Rand proposes having an ever-active mind that is willing to examine ideas critically as opposed to a "wide open mind" that is perpetually skeptical with no firm convictions "granting plausibility to everything."[26] She also touts the importance of morality without clearly defining what that morality is or should be, other than "man's life is the standard of morality, but your own life is its purpose."[27]

One of the ironies of Rand is her critique of emotions in favor of logic and yet her deep desire to extol the benefits of art is evident in her *Romantic Manifesto*. She, a successful novelist herself, well understood and appreciated that a "writer's style may project blend of reason and passionate emotion … or a chaos of floating abstractions, of emotions cut off from reality."[28]

Furthermore, achieving personal happiness stands as the highest purpose within such objectivist/rationalist ideologies. This then is a philosophy driven more by emotion than by reason. In this context, both Rand and Kant mix reason and emotion, yet they channel these faculties toward vastly different philosophical ends. Despite both philosophers claiming rational objectivity, a closer examination reveals subjective elements within both their respective philosophical frameworks. If Kant's understanding and proof of higher concepts are intuitive though, and Rand's are personal and subjective, the question arises: Whose philosophy then, if any, is right? A series of past debates (involving contemporaries of Rand), as well as more recent discussions, helps to sharpen our focus on this question.

2

The God or no God debates

"Man is a Religious Animal. He is the only Religious Animal. He is the only animal that has the True Religion — several of them. He is the only animal that loves his neighbor as himself and cuts his throat if his theology isn't straight."

~ Mark Twain

"There is only one religion, though there are a hundred versions of it."

~ *George Bernard Shaw*

A civil yet popular debate on the existence of God took place shortly after the Second World War between agnostic philosopher Bertrand Russell and Father Fredrick Copleston in a 1948 BBC radio broadcast.

Father Copleston was a Jesuit priest, who taught the history of philosophy and wrote an influential multi-volume work on the same subject. He faithfully advocated Thomas Aquinas' concept of an omnipresent God rather than a being that was hands-off after setting the chain of cause and effect into motion.

Bertrand Russell was a popular British philosopher, mathematician, and writer. His grandfather had been a prime minister and his godfather was John Stuart Mill, one of the most influential philosophers of the 19th century, proponent of individual liberty, and co-founder of modern utilitarianism.

Throughout the debate both men are respectful of one another and conduct themselves with the control and civility of two mature and seasoned college professors. Father Copleston begins by asking his opponent to accept the term God to "mean a supreme personal Being – distinct from the world, and Creator of the world," for which Russell accepts. He then asks if Russell would agree "that the problem of God is a problem of great importance," and "that if God does not exist, human beings and human history can have no other purpose than the purpose they choose to give themselves, which – in practice – is likely to mean the purpose which those impose who have the power to impose it." Russell agrees but with a caveat on Copleston's last point.[29]

Russell quotes G.E. Moore's *Principia Ethica* which maintains concepts of good and evil are definite and distinct but do not require God to support that contention. Moore, professor of philosophy at Cambridge, held that one's natural beliefs based on simple acceptance of what the senses tells us (a philosophy of common sense), are more likely to be right than complicated skepticism (a belief that all values are baseless). He, like Russell, worked effectively to undermine the then-popular idealism (or spiritualism) of Berkeley, Hume and Kant without admitting to have disproved such spiritualism. Instead they said there was no good philosophical argument that what exists is mental or spiritual.

Unable to agree whether values are relative or can be absolute without an absolute being, Copleston and Russel move onto the metaphysical questions. Metaphysics is commonly defined as that which concerns itself with the fundamental nature of reality and a study of what is "outside" objective physical experience (although a new definition for what is "alongside" the physical may presently be in order; i.e. "paraphysical"). Ontology, on the other hand, came to be that narrower branch of metaphysics which focuses more on being itself and how things that exist can be grouped according to similarities and differences (Aristotle's original metaphysics more broadly included ontology, theology, and science).

Copleston relies on Leibniz's philosophical argument to show that God exists necessarily from the theory of contingency or first causes. Leibniz, recognized as the co-founder of modern calculus (along with Newton), received his doctorate in law at age 21. He accepted earlier proofs of God but was most convinced that the best proof was "this perfect harmony of so many substances which have no communication with each other" and such surprising harmony can only come from a common cause.[30]

Father Copleston argues that God is logically necessary, as the world is a cause-and-effect world, and that the universe itself must have had a cause since every object in nature can be traced to a cause. Russell says he can conceive of the universe itself as just being and not needing a cause. Russell goes a step further and reminds Father Copleston that "physicists assure us that individual quantum transitions in atoms have no cause."[31] Father Copleston concedes that some scientists allow for indetermination within a restricted field, but such inference may be temporary. On this point Russell agrees but says at least the mind can conceive of actions without causes.

Copleston says he "cannot see how science could be conducted on any other assumption than that of order and intelligibility in nature." Russell answers that there might not be a cause, even if the scientist searches for one.

Russell adds that, "If there's a world in which most events, but not all, have causes, he will then be able to depict the probabilities and uncertainties by assuming that this particular event you're interested in probably has a cause. And since in any case you won't get more than probability that's good enough."

Copleston counters, "It may be that the scientist doesn't hope to obtain more than probability, but in raising the question he assumes that the question of explanation has a meaning," and continues, "But your general point then, Lord Russell, is that it's illegitimate even to ask the question of the cause of the world?" Russell confirms, "Yes, that's my position." Copleston requests clarification: "Well, if it's a question that for you has no meaning, it's of course very difficult to discuss it, isn't it?" Russell concedes, "Yes, it is very difficult. What do you say – shall we pass on to some other issue?"[32]

There is much that can be inferred from this debate and the differences these two proponents proffer, but more can be garnered from what they agree on. First, they agree that the question of whether God exists is important and if God does not exist then man has no purpose, other than the purpose he gives himself. Second, the predictions we make based on the world we see assumes most, if not all, events have predictable causes, but whether there is a first cause or not, the best we can hope for is probability and not certainty. Ultimately, they are unable to convincingly argue that this uncertainty is because a supreme being controls the variables, or because nature itself at some level has elements of indeterminacy.[33]

Fast forward to April 7, 2010, when another more spirited debate took place between the late atheist advocate Christopher Hitchens and a Catholic Indian-American political conservative, Dinesh D'Souza. Hitchens, a self-described Marxist conservative, was also an excellent essayist and good journalist, amongst those brave enough to speak truth to power. He strove to get to the bottom of his investigative inquiries regardless of the topic. And what subject could be more telling of man's place and purpose in the universe than God himself? If there is a hierarchy of ideas and beliefs that guide our personal and collective decisions, surely there is none higher than the belief or non-belief in God.

The debate entitled "Is Religion the Problem?" took place in the hallowed halls of today's most prestigious Catholic institution of higher learning, Notre Dame. It was not atypical of many other such recent debates between believers and non-believers, but frames common current questions of proponents for both sides. As such debates often unfold, there is the lauding up of the certainty of science, but then the tearing down of such science for its lack of purpose, leaving us in a subjective moral limbo. Unlike the Copleston-Russell debate, this one took a more cutting and competitive tone. More like a boxing match than a debate. And as is currently the case, the evolution of Darwin's evolution is fully in play. For purpose of illustration, what follows is a rough blow-by-blow summary of the exchange.

Hitchens is given the podium first and starts the debate saying religion is manmade and the result of an imperfectly evolved species. Religion is the first attempt at cosmology, he says. He quotes Darwin's reminding us of our connection to other animal species (the indelible stamp of our lowly origin) as confirmation that religion is just a first but poor attempt at describing our place in the world. He quotes evolutionary biologist Stephen Gould: "Well, these are non-overlapping magisteria, the material world, the scientific world and the faith world." Hitchens, not unlike deGrasse Tyson, believes they are not merely non-overlapping but incompatible.[34]

Hitchens reminds us that we nearly went extinct, as has almost 99% of life on earth, and we are only halfway through our solar system's lifespan. Faced with these facts, he asks how one can believe that the main events in human history occurred 2-3 thousand years ago and this was the critical time for the heavens to intervene (referring to Jesus dying on the cross as our only means to salvation). "Can you be brought to believe this? I stand before you as someone who quite simply cannot and who refuses, furthermore, to be told that if I don't believe it that I wouldn't have any source for ethics or morality."

D'Souza gingerly takes to the podium and, in response, clarifies he would not argue on the utility of religion but the truth of religion. He begins by countering with the Presuppositional argument. The cell cannot have evolved because evolution presupposes the cell. So how did we get a complex cell? A bolt of lightning in a warm pond forming a cell is preposterous. He says others, such as Richard Dawkins, proposed it came perhaps from another planet (why, because it is "the best explanation he could come up with other than Intelligent Design").

Because evolution depends on the constants of nature, if we change the constant even slightly the universe cannot exist. D'Souza quotes English physicist Stephen Hawking to remind us that if you change the rate of expansion of the universe by less than just one part in a millionth-million, we would have no universe and no life anywhere. "Why should the universe be structured in precisely this way and no other way?" He illustrates, by way of example, the anthropic principle popularized by astrophysicist Brandon Carter. Carter, in response to the Copernican principle (which states our place in the universe is not special), suggests, "Although our situation is not necessarily *central*, it is inevitably privileged to some extent."

As to the source of our moral questions, Hitchens takes his cue from Socrates and answers that it must be taken by ourselves. D'Souza counters that morality does not fit the selfish evolutionary model, nor does a self-constructed morality explain why we feel a moral law within us even when it works against us.

Here we have both men asking their opposing camps (of believers or non-believers) tough questions but providing no concrete answers. Perhaps it is as Hitchens argues in his rebuttal because belief in God is unfalsifiable. He concedes that you cannot disprove that there was a first cause and that it was godly (without conceding there is evidence of this) but insists there is no sign of an interventionist God. D'Souza however points out that neither can science answer the most basic questions such as what the purpose of life is, why we are here, where we are going, and what happens to us after we die.[35]

The debate proves thoroughly engaging, thought provoking, both men having robust jabs and volleys, but in the end neither atheism nor religion gaining the upper hand or a knockout punch. So, what can we gain or learn from these debates, if anything? If nothing else we can narrow the questions. Is religion just a poor first attempt at cosmology? Was Jesus' dying on the cross (if he was crucified at all) 2000 years ago the pivotal and critical event for all of mankind's salvation? Is evolution sufficient to explain development of the cell? Can science and religion be compatible? Can you have an objective system of morality without a supreme good, or supreme being as a guide? What is the purpose of life? Why are we here? What will happen to us after we die?

Atheism is nothing new but became more popular concurrently with the 18th century Age of Enlightenment, the French Revolution, and the growing acceptance of evolution. Today in England and Wales the non-religious are the largest growing demographic followed by Islam. Recent polls estimate 20% of the EU do not believe in "any sort of spirit, God or life force," while 61% of people in China reported that they are atheists.[36] Globally around 2% of people polled identify as convinced atheists while another 12% are irreligious.[37] Common arguments for non-belief include lack of evidence, the problem of evil (if God is good, why would he allow evil in the world), and revelations that are inconsistent with science.

Through modern debates like that with D'Souza, atheist advocates Christopher Hitchens, Richard Dawkins, Sam Harris, and Daniel Dennett came to be referred to as the four horsemen of the non-apocalypse. They represent a new secular political atheist movement that aims to counter and criticize religion (primarily Judeo-Christian-Islamic). Their ideas and critiques are well documented in a number of publications including *God is not Great: How Religion Poisons Everything* (Hitchens), *The God Delusion* (Dawkins), *Darwin's Dangerous Idea* (Dennett), and *The End of Faith: Religion, Terror, and the Future of Reason* (Harris). Let's examine briefly some of the key concepts and arguments they raise – their strengths and weaknesses – to see if they hold up to objective scrutiny, the same scrutiny they impose on the community of believers. After careful review you should find that many of their critiques and arguments are valid and well taken, while others are weak and untenable, or off base if not rationally mendacious. The same can be said of those in the community of believers for whom we shall address in later chapters.

-B-

THE INCOHERENCE OF THE NEO ATHEISTS

3

Hitchens – The case against secularism

"Religion is regarded by the common people as true, by the wise as false, and by the rulers as useful."

~ Seneca the Younger

Hitchens is the quintessential skeptic, and his skepticism is directed at western religion with a particular loathing for Christianity. In his book *God is not Great* he objects to religion because it misrepresents the origins of the cosmos which produces extensive servility, which causes dangerous sexual repression, all grounded on wishful thinking.[38] He is skeptical of whether Moses was a real historical person at all and asserts there "was no flight from Egypt, no wandering through the desert… [i]t was all, quite simply and very ineptly, made up at a much later date."[39] As for the New Testament he says, "just like the Old Testament, the 'New' one is also a work of crude carpentry, hammered together long after its purported events, and full of improvised attempts to make things come out right."[40]

Hitchens argues that the Quran is borrowed from the Jewish and Christian myths but admits that the prophet

Muhammad ﷺ (peace be upon him), unlike Moses or Jesus, was a person in ascertainable history.[41] He concedes that the Quran may have been compiled in its present form at or shortly after the life of Muhammad but that the stories (also known as hadith) surrounding the prophet are suspect, the majority of them having been compiled and translated nearly two hundred years after the events they profess to describe. He praises Jewish archaeologists who discount the historical Exodus story. He praises Jews and Christians for abandoning the rituals of antiquity (such as using only Latin and Hebrew in ritual practices), but attacks Muslims for maintaining the sanctity and primacy of the revealed text. He seems at the same time to both praise and criticize Christianity for the "immense number of possible 'Bibles'" (presumably through translation and linguistic analysis) and then criticizes Islam for not undertaking a similar "reformation."[42]

The further we recede into history the more difficult it is to verify sources and accuracy. Even so there is ample material to strongly suggest Moses was truly an actual historical figure and that an exodus from Egypt in some form did in fact take place. There is even more evidence of an historical Jesus whose activities are chronicled by the Romans. For example, the Roman Jewish historian Josephus – in his work about the antiquity of the Jews written around 93 CE – references Jesus, the brother of James, while Roman historian and Senator Tacitus references Jesus and the crucifixion around 116 CE as well. Muhammad's life and the development of the early Muslim community is well documented, if not entirely accurately preserved in every hadith (oral tradition). Hitchens is on solid ground in asserting that the Judeo-Christian religion was hammered together long after the salient events, but not in asserting that many of their primary figures are invented.

He is rather more convincing in demonstrating the "obvious fact that religion is used by those in temporal charge to invest themselves with authority." He is accurate in positing that religion kills (such as crusaders killing Muslims and heretics, Catholics killing Protestants, Palestinians and Israelis killing one another, Sunnis killing Kurds and Shiites, Shiites killing Sunnis, Muslim terrorists killing indiscriminately but mostly killing Muslims), but not in seeing that secularism kills more. Instead he staunchly defends secularism. In fact, he devotes an entire chapter to this end, anticipating "the 'Case' against secularism," knowing that the secular, atheist, totalitarian state did not have a wholly favorable humanitarian history.

Hitchens, while acknowledging that fascism, Nazism, and Stalinism are secular totalitarian regimes, does not directly address the atrocities carried out under these regimes. Rather his argument is largely an attack on the religious elements who favored or tolerated these regimes, like the Catholics' sympathy for fascism in Italy and their toleration of Hitler's oppressive rules in Germany, rather than on the regimes themselves. For instance, he highlights the French right-wing party welcoming a fascist from Germany rather than standing by their domestically elected Jewish politician, referencing Léon Blum, a socialist who led the Popular Front government. Hitchens reminds us that "when the German conquest of France arrived, these forces eagerly collaborated in the rounding up and murder of French Jews, as well as in the deportation to forced labor of huge numbers of other Frenchmen."[43] His criticism of Catholics in France is misplaced. Even though Roman Catholicism is the religion of a majority of the French people, it has not been the state religion since 1789. In fact, France today is amongst the world's most secular countries (in a 2010 Eurobarometer poll 40% of French citizens do not believe in God or some sort of spirit).[44]

A century before the atrocities of the Second World War, the most influential atheist of modern history, the 19th century Prussian philosopher and economist Karl Marx, was laying the groundwork for a radically different understanding of religion and its role in society. It was his anti-capitalist ideas and Communist Manifesto that drove communist revolutions around the world. Marx believed that religion is a manmade reaction to alienation in material life. For Marx, religion was an outlet or "protest against real suffering … the sigh of the oppressed creature, the heart of a heartless world, and the soul of soulless conditions."[45] The Marxist goal of abolishing religion was the demand for real and not illusory happiness.

The Russian October Revolution of 1917 attempted to achieve Marx's goals and unite all the people of the world in a state free of Capitalism. To affect its objective the communists confiscated church property, discouraged religion and mandated atheism in schools. Russian communism's most staunch proponent and repressive dictator was Joseph Stalin.

Raised a Greek Orthodox Christian, Joseph Stalin later became an atheist and remained so till the day he died. From the time of the Russian revolution till 1940 the number of eastern orthodox churches fell just shy of 30,000 to 500. And of the 130,000 Orthodox priests arrested during this period, 95,000 were executed. Under Stalin's brutal rule and cult of personality, an estimated 20 million people were killed. The number varies but at least 1.5 million were ordered executed, approximately 5 million died in the gulags, and about two million during deportation, with the rest attributed to neglect.[46] No one denies that Stalin was cruel, but by sheer numbers alone the self-proclaimed atheist Mao Tse Tung was even more brutal and oppressive.

Mao Tse Tung, the founding father of the People's Republic of China, was raised a Buddhist by his mother but abandoned his faith in his mid-teen years. Although he idolized the likes of George Washington and Napoleon Bonaparte, he despised Christianity as a western value. He was not religious and felt he had no duty to others. He described himself as an atheist or *wu fa wu tian* (without law and without heaven). In his early journal he wrote, "I do not agree with the view that to be moral, the motive of one's actions has to be benefiting others. Morality does not have to be defined in relation to others … People like me want to … satisfy our hearts to the full, and in doing so we automatically have the most valuable moral codes. Of course, there are people and objects in the world, but they are all there only for me … People like me only have a duty to ourselves; we have no duty to other people."[47]

Frank Dikötter, a Hong Kong historian who was allowed a rare look at early Chinese communist archives, found that the number of people who died under Mao›s regime from 1958 to 1962 alone was comparable to the Second World War: "At least 45 million people were worked, starved or beaten to death in China over these four years; the worldwide death toll of the Second World War was 55 million."[48] To put this into perspective, consider the overall death toll of the First World War was 17 million with over 20 million wounded.

Although Hitchens would suggest that most of the world's woes are the result of religious zeal, secular regimes like Stalin's and Mao's show us the limit of this hypothesis. In fact, good old-fashioned greed and power usually plays a more important role. Capitalism and its resulting international rivalries were the cause of the First World War, and its economic consequences the cause of the Second World War. While it is true the majority of constituents of the countries involved in the first and second world wars were Christian, the reasons for the wars were for purely economic interests, not religious zealotry. And while it may be true, as Hitchens suggests, that the Roman Catholic Church saw some utility in an "organic and corporate society, presided over by a leader or guide," that leader or guide has invariably been a secular political one, not a religious one.

Marshal Foch, France's top military leader before and during the First World War, wrote in December 1918, "What do we all seek? New outlets for an ever-increasing commerce and for industries which, producing far more than they can consume or sell, are constantly hampered by an increasing competition. And then? Why! New areas for trade are cleared by cannon shot. Even the Bourse [Stock Exchange], for reasons of interest, can cause armies to enter into campaign."[49] Foch's statement effectively portrays the capitalist drive for market expansion, illustrating the lengths to which nations would go, including warfare, to secure economic dominance and eliminate competition.

As we transition from early 20th century capitalism to the global stage of imperialism, we see these secular economic forces continuing to shape world events. France and England's industrial, military and naval dominance was being challenged by Germany's rapid expansion following its unification in 1871. Germany was trying to play catch up in imperialism, but the colonial game was dominated by others, particularly England. England had acquired Canada, Australia, New Zealand and India to protect its trade routes. A typical progression (particularly in Asia) was the arrival of missionaries, traders, soldiers, then a governor. In this sense Christianity was a vehicle for getting an economic foothold in Asia. Of course, there were repercussions. Christianity was viewed by some as alien and antithetical to Asian customs and culture. As a result, shortly after Mao's communist takeover of mainland China in 1949, religion was discouraged by the state and an estimated 10,000 Christian missionaries left the country in what has been politely described by some as a "reluctant exodus."

Shifting our focus to East Asia, we observe the establishment of the People's Republic of Korea by the Supreme Leader Kim Il Sung. Sung was raised a Presbyterian but appears to have abandoned any religious ideologies for more political communist ambitions.[50] Because of Kim's reforms, North Korea is an atheist state where public religion is discouraged. *Juche* is the official political ideology of North Korea, and is the holistic ideal of complete self-reliance for all North Korean individuals, which in turn is meant to uphold the sovereignty for the nation as a whole. Originally developed by Sung, it is now championed by current leadership per the regime, which repeatedly describes it as "Comrade Kim Jong-un's revolutionary thought."[51] Juche is a concept that permeates daily life for all North Koreans, who are expected to take responsibility for the success of their aspirationally global socialist revolution.[52]

North Korean communism, much the same as Russian and Chinese communism, was derived from Marxism and Leninism but with an even greater emphasis on the individual and the sovereignty of the state. Like Mao, Kim Il Sung was suspicious of Christianity which he often criticized in his writings. He believed, rightly in some respects, that religion had been used as a tool for imperialists in the Korean peninsula.

At the turn of the 20th century, the Western world was still deeply entangled in colonial rivalries, vying for economic dominance on a global scale. This context provides a backdrop to understand Kim's skepticism towards foreign influences. One striking example of these colonial power plays was the German support for the Boers (early Dutch and German settlers in Africa) in mineral-rich South Africa to undermine the control of the British. In 1936, Dr. Heinrich Schnee – previously the colonial governor of German East Africa – wrote, "The colonies offer an assured market for our own industrial produce; they afford a field of investment for the savings and capital of the Mother country." But the real rising star following the First World War was America, not Germany. America quickly became England's biggest rival, and the greatest object of their rivalry was oil.[53]This aggressive scramble for resources underscores the moral ambiguity inherent in secular capitalism. Historian Howard Zinn captures the silent economic warfare:

> Quietly, behind the headlines in battles and bombings, American diplomats and businessmen worked hard to make sure that when the war ended, American economic power would be second to none in the world. United States business would penetrate areas that up to this time had been dominated by England. The Open Door Policy of equal access would be extended from Asia to Europe, meaning that the United States intended to push England aside and move in. Before the war was over, the administration was planning the outlines of the new international economic order, based on partnership between government and big business.[54]

Roosevelt's Secretary of State Cordell Hull, at the beginning of the war, openly acknowledged this economic ambition: "Leadership toward a new system of international relationships in trade and other economic affairs will devolve very largely upon the United States because of our great economic strength. We should assume this leadership, and the responsibility that goes with it, primarily for reasons of pure national self-interest."[55]

British journalist Anthony Sampson noted, "By the end of the war the dominant influence in Saudi Arabia was unquestionably the United States. King Ibn Saud was regarded no longer as a wild desert warrior, but as a key piece in the power-game, to be wooed by the West. Roosevelt, on his way back from Yalta in February 1954, entertained the King..."[56] This transition of power in strategic regions like the Middle East further highlights the secular motivations driving international relations during this period.

Assistant Secretary of State and poet Archibald MacLeish expressed his disillusionment with America's trajectory post-war: "As things are now going, the peace we will make, the peace we seem to be making, will be a peace of oil, a peace of gold, a peace of shipping, a peace, in brief ... without moral purpose or human interest..."[57] MacLeish's concern here serves as a poignant reminder of the ethical blind spots that can arise when secular ideologies prioritize economic gain.

The trend toward secular economic interest with little thought to moral repercussions only grew after the Second World War.

A perfect illustration of this was the secular interests of Communist China and capitalist America in Vietnam and Indochina. An estimated 6 million people were killed, wounded or displaced in Vietnam and Cambodia. General Westmoreland's war of attrition was made possible by Secretary of State Henry Kissinger's implementation of the dropping of 3.7 million tons of bombs in Indochina between 1969 and 1973 (almost double the total munitions dropped in WW2).

Ironically even Christopher Hitchens agrees Mr. Kissinger should be indicted for war crimes, which include as Zinn reveals, "the deliberate mass killing of civilian populations in Indochina and the personal suborning and planning of murder of a senior constitutional officer in a democratic nation – Chile – with which the United States was not at war."[58] Kissinger is described by Hitchens as a Machiavellian politician no better than the likes of Mao or Stalin, only clothed in legal and democratic regalia. Capitalist and communist regimes, although differing in their ideologies, are at their core secular in nature. Neither have hesitated to engage in violence when it serves their ideological, political, or financial objectives

Marx said that "religion is the opiate of the masses" and a tool to placate the working class and keep them docile as a means of exploitation. Napoleon Bonaparte, a Roman Catholic, similarly asserted, "Religion is excellent stuff for keeping common people quiet. Religion is what keeps the poor from murdering the rich." Napoleon, unlike Marx though, saw religion, at least Christianity, as the basis of all advanced civilization. He believed Catholicism with its top-down hierarchical nature was best suited for maintaining order and morality. Conversely he believed Protestantism, with its emphasis on individual interpretation, more susceptible to sewing discord and disagreements.

Thus Marx, the man indirectly responsible for inspiring some of the most brutal regimes in modern times, also has the reputation for being "history's most famous atheist" (except arguably Egypt's pharaoh during Moses' time). And indeed, when Lenin and Mao finally put Marxism on the map, they banned religion from the mainstream communist world.

While many wars have been waged "in the name of religion," a thorough examination of history reveals that the majority are actually motivated by secular, geo-political, and economic interests, with religious adherents often manipulated as their pawns. A close study of 20th century conflicts reveals a recurring pattern, battles waged for purely secular ambitions, culminating in a tragic and staggering loss of life. The end result? By even the most conservative estimates, over 100 million deaths in the 20th century alone. Religions sometimes kill, but Atheism and Secularism kill much much more.

4
Harris – Violence is non-denominational

"Men will wrangle for religion; write for it; fight for it; die for it; anything but live for it."

~ C.C. Colton (1780–1832)

There are two large underlying assumptions regarding religion and science that are incorrect. One is that to be a scientist or one who seeks objective truths and empirical knowledge, that you cannot believe in God or be spiritual. The other is that religion itself discourages mutual scientific inquiry and the pursuit of truth and knowledge.

Sam Harris in his book, *The End of Faith*, like his fellow neo atheists, spares no criticism of religion and faith, believing them to be built on outdated, unsubstantiated myths. He is critical because he perceives them as practiced by a "culture that has elevated belief, in the absence of evidence, to the highest place in the hierarchy of human virtues ... and every child is instructed that it is, at the very least, an option, if not a sacred duty, to disregard the facts of this world out of deference to the God who lurks in his mother's and father's imaginations."[59] We believe what we believe, he correctly points out, due mostly to what others have told us, both ordinary people and experts. He recommends that we form our beliefs on the basis of the best evidence, not merely on what most people or a higher authority may believe.

Harris, like Hitchens, briefly tries to distinguish the brutality of Mao and Stalin whose "communism was little more than a political religion."[60] This is a mischaracterization and downplays the role secular, anti-religious philosophies play in real world political maneuvering. Although people are killed regularly by what someone else believes in God, as Harris states, it is not the principal cause of armed conflict as any cursory examination of world history reveals. On this point Harris can be forgiven for he doesn't defend secularism as much as he attacks Judaism, Christianity, and particularly Islam.

Harris quotes Deuteronomy 13:12-16 as an inquisitor's justification for killing anyone who professes sympathy to a foreign god. He considers the early problem of anti-Semitism directed against Jews stemmed in part "for their refusal to assimilate, for the insularity and professed superiority of their religious culture."[61] As a belief, without the easy conversions allowed in Christianity and Islam, he sees Judaism as the least suited to survive and that it "remains a lightning rod for intolerance to this day." Judaism, he says, is:

> as intrinsically divisive, as ridiculous in its literalism and at odds with the civilizing insights of modernity as any other religion. Jewish Settlers, by exercising their "freedom of belief" on contested land, are now one of the principal obstacles to peace in the Middle East. They will be a direct cause of war between Islam and the West should one ever erupt over the Israeli-Palestinian conflict.[62]

To say Judaism is at odds with the civilizing insights of modernity is rather dismissive of the key role played by Judaism and the Jewish people in their assimilation into the Western world, and in turn their help in assimilation of the Western world into what it is today. However, to say that modern Zionism and its supporters could be the primary cause of war between Islam and the West is not without merit. Harris reinforces this notion, remarking, "Fundamentalist Christians support Israel because they believe that the final consolidation of Jewish power in the Holy Land – specifically the rebuilding of Solomon's temple – will usher in both the Second Coming of Christ and the final destruction of the Jews."

Harris sees 1st century Christians as a minority Jewish sect who believed Jesus was the messiah (Greek: Christos) while the majority did not. He remarks that only Matthew and Luke describe Jesus as being from a virgin birth and that it may have been inspired by a mistranslation of an Old Testament Hebrew word "*almah*" which means "young woman," but when translated into Greek as "*parthenos*" means "virgin." The biblical prophet Isaiah, in roughly the 8th century BCE, promised the king of Judah that a young woman (almah) would give birth to a child named Immanuel who would hearken the end of the king's enemies (Isaiah 7:14-17). He notes that there is no credible evidence that Jesus ever saw himself as anything but "a Jew among Jews, seeking the fulfillment of Judaism…" Harris laments that this so-called miracle of the virgin birth, coupled with those that Jesus is purported to have performed, is "solid and palpable" proof for even so nimble a mind as mathematician and physicist Blaise Pascal.[63]

Where Harris sees in the Old Testament justification for Christians killing witches, Jews, Muslims and heretics, he sees in the New Testament an additional justification for anti-Semitism. "For ye like things of your own countrymen, even as they have of the Jews: who both killed the Lord Jesus, and their own prophets, and have persecuted us; and they please not God, and are contrary to all men" (Thessalonians 2:14-16). From this perspective, the destruction of the temple in 70 CE and the displacement of the Jews was proof that Jesus was, in fact, the messiah and the consequence of not accepting him as such. While Harris acknowledges German Nazism was anti-Christian and their anti-Semitism secularly motivated, he finds dormant in early Christianity a strain of anti-Semitism developed in Rome and the Catholic Church that persisted throughout Europe.[64] The salient fact that should not be lost, though, is that the horrific genocide enacted upon the Jewish people was done at the behest of an anti-Christian, secular, racially and non-religously motivated movement and ideology.[65]

Harris acknowledges that Muslims made many important contributions to science "at a time when European Christians were luxuriating in the most abysmal ignorance." But "people of faith have created almost everything of value in our world," he says, because before the 20th century there was "simply no one else to do the job."[66] Notwithstanding this singular compliment to Muslims, Harris has an open disdain for Islam and Muslims in much the same way Hitchens does for Christianity and Christians. The first pages of his book describe a fictitious suicide bomber on a public bus who inevitably must be Muslim (apparently only Muslims could perform such an act).

Harris devotes an entire chapter to the "problem with Islam" and says it, unlike Jainism, is a religion filled with bad beliefs. There is nothing in Jainists' beliefs, he suggests, that would inspire them to commit suicidal acts of terrorism like those of Muslims.[67] Here Harris misses the mark in more ways than one. First, suicide is nowhere encouraged by tenets of Islam but is instead strongly discouraged. The Quran makes it expressly forbidden: "and do not kill yourselves, surely God is most merciful to you" (Surah 4:29). Similarly, numerous hadith and Imams, both Sunni and Shia, describe a torment in hell for this ungracious act.[68]

Second, Jainism and Buddhism are branches of a yet more ancient Indian religious tradition whose central tenet is nonviolence and respect toward all living beings. Yet Muslims have a long history being persecuted in Burma from the first Taoungoo dynasties (whose kings were patrons of Buddhism) up to the recent murder of 200 Muslims spurned by anti-Muslim pamphlets distributed by Buddhist monks in Taoungoo in 2001. These killings were followed by the destruction of 11 mosques and arson of over 400 Muslim homes, with repeated and similar attacks occurring right up to the present day. In fact, Rohingya Muslims are the most persecuted minority group in the world, according to Amnesty International. At the hands of Myanmar's Buddhist majority, they are regularly subjected to discrimination, rape, torture, arbitrary detention, and violence. These incidents often go unreported because the assailants include not only local civilians but law enforcement and military authorities as well.[69]

Jainism practices includes Sallekhana, one of the last vows of Jain ethical code, which, although not technically suicide, requires gradually reducing food and liquids at the end of one's life. The Rajasthan High Court banned the practice in 2015, calling it suicide, but the Supreme Court of India stayed the ban later that same year. So, no, Muslims are not any more predisposed to committing suicide than Jainists, nor are they more violent. In truth, many revered Jain kings were conquerors of peoples and territories even though the core tenets of Jainism instruct conquering oneself, just as Islam teaches that the greater jihad is the one within, not on any battlefield. These concepts are not at odds with one defending oneself.

Modern biblical scholar and political commentator Reza Aslan does not believe that Christianity and Judaism are necessarily any less prone to promoting violence than Islam, but believes instead one's socio-political and economic circumstances are a much greater indicator for extremists or radical views than any core texts of Judaism, Christianity or Islam.

In a debate with Aslan, Sam Harris suggests that Judaism and Christianity have tempered their violent aspects and Islam has not. Aslan disagrees, citing priests taking up arms and murdering opponents in 1980s Latin America in the name of Jesus as just one example. A Muslim growing up in a garbage heap in Gaza has a different religious worldview than one growing up in an affluent neighborhood of L.A., says Aslan.

In the debate Harris cites a Pew poll that finds 77% of Muslims in Lebanon justify suicide bombing. The poll itself in fact found only 9% reported it is often justified, not 77%. Instead, 66% found it is rarely or never justified. The question itself, according to the poll, is "Do you feel suicide bombing and other forms of violence to defend Islam from its enemies is often justified?" The question is ambiguous in we do not know if they are referring to violence other than suicide bombing, and also whether they are answering that others often justify violence or that they themselves believe such acts are justified.[70] Harris assumes that Bin Laden's attacks on the World Trade Center were motivated primarily by theological concerns. Aslan disagrees, citing Bin Laden's own justification for the attacks, including Palestine, troops in Saudi Arabia, and the situation in Iraq.[71] Neither Aslan nor Harris, though, dispute that religion is used by the politically and personally ambitious to secure power and control.

Harris acknowledges that he ignores the "roots of Muslim violence," such as "the painful history of the Israeli occupation ... the collusion of Western powers with corrupt dictatorships ... the endemic poverty and lack of economic opportunity that now plague the Arab world." But he argues he can ignore these things because "the world is filled with poor, uneducated, and exploited peoples who do not commit acts of terrorism..." He says, "We are at war with Islam," because it is "the vision of life prescribed to all Muslims in the Koran, and further elaborated in the literature of the hadith..."[72]

Harris, without explanation, states that Islam is divided into a "House of Islam" and a "House of War," and that Islam is a religion of conquest, which is misleading. First, there is no precise definition in the Quran or hadith of either "*Dar al Islam*" or "*Dar al Harb*," and thus it is not a core belief. These concepts developed only after the growth of the Umayyad and Abbasid dynasties, which required them to establish political and international relationships with their neighbors. Second, when these early dynasties began entering into treaties with nearby kingdoms, they developed the concept of *Dar al Aman* or "house of safety" as well. Moreover, the Quran itself, Surah 9:4 and 60:8, directs Muslims to honor their covenants with non-Muslims and if they incline to peace to treat them with kindness.[73]

Harris further states, again without support, "The only future devout Muslims can envisage – *as Muslims* – is one in which all infidels have been converted to Islam, subjugated, or killed."[74] This is a gross mischaracterization of the tenets of Islam, which refers to anyone who believes in God, or one God generally, as a Muslim and refers respectfully to Christians and Jews as people of the book. Further, countless passages confirm that, although it is encouraged to correctly inform others of the tenets of Islam, people will believe or not believe as God sees fit, not as its proponents see fit.

Non-Muslims, even the statue-worshiping, pagan tribes – including the Quraish with whom Muhammad was affiliated – interacted peaceably with early Muslims in both Mecca and Medina, and beyond.[75] This is evident in the treaty of Hudaybiyyah and the first Medina Constitution. The charter of Medina, drafted shortly after Muhammad's relocation to Medina from Mecca in 622 CE, was created to maintain peace amongst the many diverse tribes and codify freedom of religious beliefs. It guaranteed representation of all parties, Muslim or non-Muslim, for consultation of affairs of the state or in negotiation with foreign states. It is a unique and rare example of an early constitutionally codified state-representational democracy. Six years after the charter, Muslims from Medina were refused entry by the pagan Quraish tribe into Mecca to perform their religious pilgrimage, even though they came unarmed. By negotiation the parties agreed to a ten-year peace treaty.

It is clear that Islam and its adherents practice and envision continued human interactions amongst those who believe in God and those who do not, preferably living peacefully side by side. But unlike those who characterize Christianity as a religion that encourages turning the other cheek, Muslims do not apologize for being prepared (which is becoming increasingly rare) to defend themselves and, although discouraged, are permitted to take an eye for an eye. A review of the history of Judaism and their many exploits, as well as Christianity since the time of Constantine, will show that the Jewish and Christian people, too, did not always turn the other cheek.

The attacks reserved for Islam then seem all the more peculiar considering Harris openly admits that the key tenets of Judaism and Christianity have been relied on for wholesale institutionalized murder of anyone who professes a different religion. On the other hand, Islam actually prohibits any compulsion in religion, and has clearly defined rules for laws of land warfare, which Harris, like many others, cites incorrectly or out of context.[76] It seems the special disdain reserved for Islam and not Judaism and Christianity are because Harris, like Hitchens, sees the latter having long ago abandoned the core tenets of their faith and is thus hoping, not praying, Muslims will do the same. So, if Islam and Christianity and Judaism are not good beliefs and guides for our moral compasses, then what is?

Harris is critical of moral relativists who believe "all cultural practices should be respected on their own terms" and not judged by our Western standards, because this presumes cultural diversity is "better" than bigotry.[77] He is also critical of pragmatists and pacifists (even though he may favor Jainism). Instead he believes taking the happiness of others into account is a good way to augment one's own happiness. He says the connection between "spirituality... and ethics is well attested."[78] In light of this, inexplicably, he still argues firmly that the use of torture for exigent circumstances – for America's war on terror, for example – should not only be permissible but is necessary.[79]

Harris admits that most scientists consider themselves physicalists who "believe that our mental and spiritual lives are wholly dependent upon the workings of our brain," and yet he concedes "that nothing about a brain, when surveyed as a physical system, declares it to be a bearer of that peculiar, interior dimension that each of us experiences as consciousness in his own case." Most physicalists believe our being ceases when we die, but Harris, to the contrary, candidly admits "we simply do not know what happens after death."[80]

Harris, after thoroughly lambasting religion, ironically makes a surprising and unexpected turn in the closing chapter of his book. He advocates for mysticism and spirituality through meditation. He says it is easy to imagine that "a creature could form a representation of the world without forming a representation of *itself* in the world," which is what many spiritual practitioners do. He emphasizes the loss of subject-object perception of the kind many Buddhist texts encourage, and astutely observes, "The roiling mystery of the world can be analyzed with concepts (this is science), or it can be experienced free of concepts (this is mysticism)."[81]

Harris encourages us to turn to non-dualistic empirical mysticism which appears to have only arisen in Asia. He speculates that the Jewish, Christian, and Muslim emphasis on faith is responsible for this lack of non-dualistic spirituality, and sees the founders of the western philosophical and theological traditions to pale in comparison to the great philosophers and mystics of the East.[82] He believes "spiritual experience, ethical behavior, and strong communities are essential for human happiness" and seeks "to bring reason, spirituality, and ethics together in our thinking about the world."[83] Harris seems to at once applaud and encourage Western culture to vanquish Middle Eastern Islamic beliefs (and all Judeo-Christian beliefs for that matter), while concurrently deriding such Western culture and traditions which he sees as somehow inferior to Eastern mysticism. It is true that the history of Western thought has taken a more classical, analytical bent than a more romantic, holistic, even mystical course more commonly seen in Eastern philosophies. However, Western philosophy does not abandon wholesale belief for scientific inquiry.

5

Dawkins – Simple things can slowly make complex things

> *"Science without religion is lame, religion without science is blind."*
>
> ~ Albert Einstein

In the preface to Richard Dawkins' book, *The God Delusion,* he notes that if you are religious it is probably because of childhood indoctrination. However, Dawkins, just as everyone else, is no less immune from childhood indoctrination. The first chapter of the book, which briefly discusses the author's own childhood influences, is entitled, "A Deeply Religious Non-believer." It ponders how the rational-minded Anglican chaplain at his school could have chosen the priesthood while he did not. Dawkins freely admits that, had this Anglican chaplain read Darwin's *Origin of Species*, he "might have been led to Darwin's view that all was 'produced by laws acting around us.'"[84]

Belief in modern tenets of science, as Dawkins hints, may instruct beliefs not unlike other religious articles of faith. Science is no less a system of faith, worship and veneration than any other religious system. As a result, Dawkins goes to great lengths to make sure that one of science's most distinguished saints, Albert Einstein, is not maligned, nor reputation sullied, by the believing infidels.

Whatever Einstein's views, however, he was certainly not an atheist. He chided a personal anthropomorphic God but not God altogether. He, himself raised a secularist Jew, at age 12 liberated himself from the Jewish religious conventions of his days; he later was critical of the Bible as a collection of problematic interpretations far removed from any original texts and not necessarily the original text itself. In response to a book by a prominent Jewish philosopher of his day, Einstein wrote:

> The word God is for me nothing more than the expression and product of human weaknesses, the Bible a collection of honorable, but still primitive legends which are nevertheless pretty childish. No interpretation no matter how subtle can (for me) change this. These subtilised interpretations are highly manifold according to their nature and have almost nothing to do with the original text.

Per Prince Hubertus, Einstein said, "In view of such harmony in the cosmos which I, with my limited human mind, am able to recognize, there are yet people who say there is no God. But what really makes me angry is that they quote me for the support of such views."[85]

Einstein is commonly quoted as saying, "I want to know how God created this world. I am not interested in this or that phenomenon, in the spectrum of this or that element. I want to know His thoughts; the rest are details"[86] and "Everyone who is seriously involved in the pursuit of science becomes convinced that a spirit is manifest in the laws of the Universe – a spirit vastly superior to that of man, and one in the face of which we with our modest powers must feel humble."[87] And perhaps more famously, "God does not play dice with the universe."[88] Einstein believed in a God or spirit, but apparently not in any anthropomorphic God we may be familiar with.

In an interview during which Einstein was asked about whether he was a pantheist, he responded:

> Your question is the most difficult in the world. It is not a question I can answer simply with yes or no. I am not an Atheist. I do not know if I can define myself as a Pantheist. The problem involved is too vast for our limited minds. ... We see a universe marvelously arranged, obeying certain laws, but we understand the laws only dimly. Our limited minds cannot grasp the mysterious force that sways the constellations. I am fascinated by Spinoza's Pantheism. I admire even more his contributions to modern thought. Spinoza is the greatest of modern philosophers, because he is the first philosopher who deals with the soul and the body as one, not as two separate things.[89]

Baruch Spinoza was a 17th century Dutch Jewish philosopher and lens crafter who was banned by members of the local Jewish community at age 23 for questioning the nature of God and the credibility of scripture, particularly the Hebrew Bible.

Spinoza's deterministic cause-and-effect views were no doubt appealing to Einstein. Spinoza said in his *Ethics*, "Whatsoever is, is in God, and without God nothing can be, or be conceived" and "Although each particular thing be conditioned by another particular thing to exist in a given way, yet the force whereby each particular thing perseveres in existing follows from the eternal necessity of God's nature." Also appealing was Spinoza's perception of the continual and timeless act of being: "For the eternal and infinite Being, which we call God or Nature, acts by the same necessity as that whereby it exists. … Therefore, as he does not exist for the sake of an end, so neither does he act for the sake of an end; of his existence and of his action there is neither origin nor end."[90] Einstein discovered a profound resonance with Spinoza's deterministic worldview and his perception of God, which helped shape his own perceptions of the universe and its timeless laws.

In a letter of condolence to the family of his friend and mentor, Einstein wrote, "Now he has departed from this strange world a little ahead of me. That means nothing. People like us, who believe in physics, know that the distinction between past, present and future is only a stubbornly persistent illusion." As to the notion that science can inform ethics, Einstein in response to the question posed by J.W.N. Sullivan in a 1930 interview responded, "science cannot teach men to be moral and every attempt to reduce ethics to scientific formulae must fail." Spinoza, in much the same way as Socrates, said, "The mind's highest good is the knowledge of God, and the mind's highest virtue is to know God."[91]

This interest in the nature of the soul and body, and the universe and moral objective truths, was not unique to the inquiries of Einstein and Spinoza but has been a spirited topic of debate for thousands of years. Even further, certainly since the time man first walked upright and trained his head to the heavens and pondered his place in the cosmos, then looked back down to contemplate his place among men.

Plato, a 5th century BCE Greek philosopher and mathematician, founded the first known institution of higher learning in the West.

He believed in a dual reality comprised of a world in which we live and experience and a nonphysical world or realm made up of archetypal forms. Our world consisting of numerous combinations of more essential or primary prototype forms. The forms themselves are abstract properties or qualities such as roundness, hardness, redness, orangeness, etc. What we see is an imperfect image or manifestation of the original form and thus imperfect, whereas the original forms are timeless and unchanging. The objects we observe in this physical world are constantly changing. Our material world is similar to the more real and perfect world of forms. The highest form is the form of the good which is the most general and leads to the more particular, and from more objective to more subjective.

This Greek notion of another perfect realm is believed by some to have strongly influenced the Christian concept of heaven. Plato's philosophy came out of a desire to answer the question of why the world appears to be both permanent and changing, and how one can live a happy, fulfilling life when ultimately everything we cling to is transitory, including our and our loved ones' lives. It also attempted to answer the all too familiar ethical question, Can there be objective moral truths or are they just man-made conventions? Plato himself was not completely convinced of his own theory, finding it hard to reconcile the problem of having these independent, unchanging forms existing independently separated from the changing objects of our sensory world.

Plato also believed in a duality of body and soul. He believed that the soul was encapsulated in a human body departing at death to return back to the realm of the forms and then back to the human body in a continuous cycle. Socrates, as related through various Plato dialogues, purports to have believed in an immortal soul as well, deduced by the theory of recollection in which we possess some non-empirical knowledge at birth, suggesting that the soul is the vehicle for carrying that knowledge.

Plato's student, Aristotle, also believed in a body and soul but insisted that one could not exist without the other, that they were intertwined. However, for Aristotle the actualizing cause of the form of the person (the soul), exists before it is connected to the body and will exist after it perishes. Aristotle did not embrace prototype forms for particulars, but he in some sense embraced a transcendent and immanent active or prototype intellect.The form of the soul manifests itself in particular living things including humans. But whereas Plato believed in the soul's transmigration after death, Aristotle did not. At most, Aristotle contemplated an eternal mind or intellect that was a sort of wellspring of thinking or intellectual potential. By some references in this eternal intellect we have an immortal connection to our human soul, and by others it is separate.

Regardless of their nuances, the earliest founders of modern western philosophy and thought – with science and rational inquiry at its center – were themselves not atheist in any modern sense of the term. Yes, Socrates himself was sentenced to death for denying the Greek gods, but he was by no stretch of the imagination an atheist. Nor was his student Plato or Plato's student, Aristotle (who embraced metaphysical concepts like an unmoved Mover and transcendent Intellect, if not a personal creator).

Dawkins, like Harris, can apologize for the likes of Plato, Aristotle, and Newton because that's just the way things were before modern advancements in science, archeology and biology. Dawkins concedes that many of sciences' greatest contributors were religious, but finds the high mark and turning point to be the 19th century where, armed with the theory of evolution, "there was less social and judicial pressure than in earlier centuries to profess religion and more scientific support for abandoning it."[92] Never mind that some of the world's most brilliant scientific proponents have not abandoned such a worldview.

He not only takes aim at those who hold such a view but also those, like the late evolutionary biologist and science historian Stephen Jay Gould, for their view that the magisterium of science "covers the empirical realm" while the "magisterium of religion extends over questions of ultimate meaning and moral value" and "These two magisteria do not overlap."[93] Dawkins may well be right that yes, they do or should overlap at some level, and yet, like Hitchens, is wrong that they are strictly incompatible. Dawkins is not content with merely accepting that because religion is the topic of inquiry that we should hold such inquiry to a lesser standard than any other scientific inquiry. Here his argument is well taken but his vexation appears to lie more in his inability to recognize Gould's gentle humility and openness over the confidence

Dawkins has in his own fundamental atheism. Perhaps, though, by recognizing the limitations we have in undertaking such broad and pointed inquiries yet accepting the challenge of finding better answers and proofs, we can come to understand that some overlap exists. Or better yet, that no overlap exists at all because under the right lens it turns out science and religion, art and beauty, are completely compatible, having sprung from the same fountainhead. As Ptolemy Tompkins puts it, truth is like a mountain with one peak: "If all paths on that mountain lead upward then sooner or later, all those paths will end up at the same place."[94]

Dawkins runs down the weakness in various arguments in support of God but gives special thrift to the argument from improbability. He uses Fred Hoyle's Boeing 747 simile in which "Hoyle said that the probability of life originating on Earth is no greater than the chance that a hurricane, sweeping through a scrapyard, would have the luck to assemble a Boeing 747." To this Dawkins responds, like his atheist colleague Daniel Dennet, that "evolution counters one of the oldest ideas we have: 'the idea that it takes a big fancy smart thing to make a lesser thing.'"[95] Dawkins disregards the theory that God is the designer of life and the universe because then one inevitably asks who designed God. He then addresses the argument for irreducible complexity, also known as the problem of statistical improbability for complex life to have formed on its own, by offering natural selection as the simple solution. The reason why it is so simple a solution is because "natural selection is a cumulative process, which breaks the problem of improbability up into small pieces"; advocates of intelligent design, he insists, simply do not understand the power of accumulation.[96] But even Dawkins acknowledges that each of the small pieces is, if not highly, at least slightly improbable. And statistically there is still a problem.

Creationists ask, what is the use of half an eye or half a wing? And how do we get something as complex as an eye anyway. Both Darwin and Dawkins answer by gradual degrees. A cataract patient who has half their visibility could still see enough to not fall off a cliff, and half a wing could save you from falling off a tree, says Dawkins. And by extension, he says, you could see some utility in 25% of visibility or a wing, or 10%, 5%, etc. Still Dawkins agrees and Darwin conceded, "If it could be demonstrated that any complex organ existed which could not possibly have been formed by numerous, successive, slight modifications, my theory would absolutely break down, but I can find no such case."[97]

These gradual changes or slight modifications, though, are not exactly as Darwin predicted. Gould, who on the one hand has been accused of being a theist apologetic, is on the other hand regarded by many as one of the most respected evolutionary biologists since Darwin. He, along with paleontologist Niles Eldredge, published a landmark paper which showed that the degree of gradual speciation commonly attributed to Darwin is virtually nonexistent in the fossil record, which shows stasis of species is the norm with rare and geologically rapid events of branching speciation. Dawkins does not entirely disagree; he instead directs his focus on how evolution occurs at the genetic level instead of large, relatively sudden changes like those you see in the Cambrian explosion, preceded and followed by long periods of stasis. One focuses on selection and competition of different organisms, while the other is focused on selection and competition among organisms of the same species.

Dawkins levels many of the same attacks made by Hitchens and Harris against Judaism, Christianity and Islam, even citing Harris on the latter. Since they are essentially of the same variety and character, it is not necessary to address them here in detail. Dawkins does not disparage Jews and Judaism so much as he does Christians and Muslims, but he does disparage them and their religion nonetheless. Maybe in an effort to reform himself while speaking to *The New Republic* in 2013 about the high percentage of Jews winning Nobel prizes in science, he curiously replied, "Race does not come into it. It is pure religion and culture. Something about the cultural tradition of Jews is way, way more sympathetic to science and learning and intellectual pursuits than Islam."[98] This compliment, if it was meant to be one, seems contrary to his attack on religion altogether, including Christianity and especially Islam, which has been accused of simply borrowing from Judaism. A clue to this seeming contradiction comes from his chapters on the roots of religion, which suggest we have "a natural predisposition to embrace religious ideas." These same themes are explored in rather more detail by Daniel Dennett in his book *Darwin's Dangerous Idea*.

So, what is it about this theory of evolution that appears to single-handedly dispatch and do away with a millennium or more of a somewhat homogeneous (albeit garbled), sometimes simplistic, belief in God (and gods)?

6

Dennett – A valueless unfolding of nature

"The mystery of the beginning of all things is insoluble by us; and I for one must be content to remain an agnostic."

~ Charles Darwin

"Just as a candle cannot burn without fire, men cannot live without a spiritual life."

~ Buddha

In the opening chapter of his book *Darwin's Dangerous Idea*, American philosopher and cognitive scientist Daniel Dennett III realizes not all scientists and philosophers are atheist, but that if they do believe their God is not an anthropomorphic, handicrafter God. He recognizes that there are also those who ground their highest concerns in entirely secular philosophies "that stave off despair without the aid of any concept of a Supreme Being – other than the universe itself." But in the end, he understands, "What both groups share, in spite of the differences in their deepest creeds, is a conviction that life does have meaning, that goodness matters."[99]

As the title suggests, Darwin's theory was a revolutionary idea "not of the idea of evolution, but the idea of evolution by natural selection."[100] Darwin effectively showed that, contrary to conventional thinking, species are not immutable but evolve. This natural selection he proposed took place and continues to take place through a mindless, mechanical, algorithmic process. An idea or theory not fully understood or accepted by his contemporaries (nor by some yet today), hence Darwin's "dangerous idea."

Dennett perceptively points out this idea, although brilliantly simple, was revolutionary in that it began almost at once to reconstruct the traditional structure of human thought which he (Dennett) calls the Cosmic Pyramid in which mind or intelligence precedes design. Instead, Darwin claimed that "the various processes of natural selection, in spite of their underlying mindlessness, are powerful enough to have done all the design work that is manifest in the world."[101] Part of the problem with the idea was that it had implications for more than just species or biology. By extension it could be applied (and has with considerable success and failure) to other areas as well, such as psychology, cosmology, culture and sociology, ethics, politics and – a possible deal-breaker – religion.

Dennett realizes that because Darwin's idea has the power to unite and explain just about everything, it also has the power to explain away and erode the minds, purposes and meanings we hold so dear. A "universal acid" that, once it passes "through the monuments we cherish, they will cease to exist, dissolved in an unrecognizable and unlovable puddle of scientific destruction." But alas, Dennett poignantly points out this fear is unfounded, for surely:

> a proper reductionist explanation of these phenomena would leave them still standing but just demystified, unified, placed on more secure foundations. We might learn some surprising or even shocking things about these treasures, but unless our valuing these things was based on confusion or mistaken identity, how could increased understanding of them diminish their value in our eyes?[102]

Dennett suggests that meaning, like species, evolves so "*importance itself*, like everything else that we treasure, gradually evolves from nothingness" and that "the only meaning there can be is the meaning" we create for ourselves.[103] Dennett, like many of his contemporary atheists, sees God and religion also as an evolutionary process. The handicrafter God of old is now nearly extinct in the face of mindless algorithmic design, as is the notion of God as lawgiver in the wake of newly discovered Newtonian laws of nature.

Dennett concedes respectfully that religions "have brought the comfort of belonging and companionship to many who would otherwise have passed through this life all alone ... and ennobled the attitudes and refreshed the spirits of the world-beset." As well, religion, he freely admits, has unintentionally "kept *Homo sapiens* civilized enough, for long enough, for us to have learned how to reflect more systematically and accurately our position in the universe."[104]

This is an important point that bears repeating. The very thing the rational atheist scientist rails against helped make their very vocation possible. And there still remains the problem of morals or meaning being anything but subjective. Dennett admits, "Ethical decision-making, examined from the perspective of Darwin's dangerous idea, holds out scant hope of our ever discovering a formula or an algorithm for doing right." The best Dennett and others can propose in these regards is some sort of undefined utilitarianism and console us that "we have the mind-tools we need to design and redesign ourselves, ever searching for better solutions to the problems we create for ourselves and others."[105]

For Aristotle, morality was a matter of being an excellent human being, the best human being you can. Aristotle said in his essay on ethics, "Excellence or virtue is a settled disposition of the mind that determines our choice of actions and emotions and consists essentially in observing the mean relative to us ... a mean between two vices, that which depends on excess and that which depends on defect."[106] In such a moral system, the motivation for upright behavior is not based on divine commands but in striving for excellence by functioning optimally as a human being.

After the gradual consolidation of Christianity in the West, there was a decline in its influence as a moral guide and authority in the postmodern era. The German philosopher Nietzsche, upon carefully observing and documenting this decline, found the personal courage to boldly declare the death of god. Many of those who agreed with Nietzsche's assessment also worried that, without any absolute objective values, there could be no real values at all.

Nietzsche agreed, sort of. He was quick to chastise anyone who professed that any values of Christianity or the Enlightenment – or any other system – were anything more than just an arbitrary set of values developed and promulgated due to the ever-changing historical and philosophical circumstances.

Although Nietzsche was quite effective at deconstructing old assumed values, particularly the Christian ones he found so loathing, at least he was interested in building and promoting new ones. In this regard he was fond of a brilliant and courageous superhuman who could come along and construct such values based on what he liked to imagine would be an objectively superior moral system. But in the end, he nor any other superhuman ever proffered such a brilliant objective, secular moral system of values to replace the seemingly outdated and archaic transcendent ones that had been in such decline for so long.

Some have criticized a prevailing strain of Christianity, since the protestant reformation, as contributing to this decline. For what kind of moral system is it that all heretofore moral prohibitions could be absolved simply by professing your belief in a deity-turned-man, who died for your sins so you yourself would not ultimately have to bear them? In such a system the personal ownership of sins and moral transgressions are eagerly and expediently done away with, only to have the vices and transgressions oft repeated. The effect being the manifestations of all the ill consequences fraught upon the individual, the couple, the family, the society, the nation without any of the guilt (once one has confessed his sin). Sometimes even allowing one to be born again (and again, and again if necessary) depending on the severity of the transgressions.

But tearing down pre-modern Christian values and tearing down possible transcendental objective values are not the same thing. Modern biblical scholarship is increasingly showing the doctrinal foundations of such a moral system academically infirm. But it also may be pointing to a more universal and comprehensive system firmly rooted in a higher power.

Most forms of secular moral systems are generally just one form or another of utilitarianism. The problem with such systems, though, is they ironically, in the end, allow one to do what one wants to do rather than what one ought to do without any guilt or angst. The secular utilitarian says that's great: What's wrong with that so long as we have the safeguard of trying to achieve, for utility's sake, the maximum amount of happiness for the maximum number of people? Kant provided the closest thing to an answer.

Kant noted that for a utilitarian, the reason an act (such as murder) is wrong, is because it does not maximize good for those involved. But it may, he observed, for the individual committing murder. Kant argued such systems are inadequate for compelling moral action against others because the imperatives on which they are based are too subjective. He offered what he thought was a better alternative, the categorical imperative which is an unconditional requirement in all circumstances: *"Act only according to that maxim whereby you can, at the same time, will that it should become a universal law."* But this sounds a lot like the golden rule (do unto others as you would have them do to you). But even this is still subjective.

Popular American novelist, Robert Pirsig, in his second philosophical semi-autobiographical novel, *Lila*, tries to formulate another kind of rational moral system. In Pirsig's system, values are placed according to the complexity and ability for dynamic change of each system in the evolutionary chain of which society and intellect are included. Such systems, although not necessarily compelling, are closer to true rational systems not based on religious doctrine. Whether they have transcendental overtones is another question. For example, he says, "It's more moral for a doctor to kill a germ than to allow the germ to kill his patient"; "It would be immoral for Hindus not to eat their cows in a time of famine, since they would be killing human beings in favor of a lower organism"; and "A nation is a higher form of evolution than a human but intellectual ideas are even higher and more dynamic forms of complexity than nations."[107] Pirsig sees in these systems (biological, social, and intellectual) a constant struggle. The society cannot exist without the biological system, and the intellect that tries to subjugate society endangers the thing that supports its very growth and survival.

Pirsig's exploration of value systems within various layers of complexity leads us to consider broader questions in ethics including consideration of normative ethics and metaethics. Normative ethics deals with what we ought to do, whereas meta ethics deals with the very foundation of ethics and morals themselves. For Nietzsche, what was right or wrong was dependent only on your own perspective; it is relative to a time, age, and need. For religious theists, what is right or wrong is objective and absolute. But even on these two extremes there is some room for a middle way.

If man is not changing, nor his nature, then they cannot be reconciled. But if man is changing and either his nature or actions are also, then so too would his value system. In such a case, if the morals upon which man is to conduct his affairs are transcendent, they could still be open to some adjustments. In the Judeo-Christian-Islamic system, for example, there are legal and dietary restrictions that we find being imposed or dropped or loosened as the history of man unfolds. But inasmuch as man's nature is fixed, they are, for the most part, the same.

In all transcendent moral systems, the rules remain pretty much the same. The golden rules still remain the golden rules. Respect parents and elders, do not lie and steal or murder, avoid cheating on your partner, promote peace not war, and strive for your own salvation. The question then is, are these rules the product of countless revisions and development by man alone and themselves arbitrary, or are they the product of an omnipotent, omnipresent, transcendent being, or a combination of both? Morals then come down to the *ought*, the *is*, and *from where*. Is there any intelligent agency that has promulgated such values beside man? If so, could this same intelligent agency be responsible for the creation of the universe? Dennett does not see any such intelligent agency in the creation of the universe or unfolding of nature, but rather a "timeless … possibility of order" and not "something intelligent but, wonder of wonders, something intelligible."[108] And yet Dennett, seeing this process as abstract and outside of time with no origin requiring explanation, still seeks explanation of the origins of the concrete universe which creates itself out of nothing or something virtually indistinguishable from nothing.

This valueless unfolding of nature, this timeless possibility of nature when stripped down to its bare essential, begins to closely resemble Eastern schools of thought and cosmology. The careful analysis, compartmentalization, and dissecting so prevalent in Western culture is in stark contrast and yet brings us full circle to the unknowable source and absolute principle underlying the universe as expressed in the Tao of the Tao Te Ching (of Chinese philosophy) or Buddhism (as it evolved from Hindu/Indian philosophy).

PART II

RELIGION: ORIGINS, AUTHENTICITY AND BASIC BELIEFS

-A-

THE EASTERN PERSPECTIVE

7

Taoism, Hinduism and Buddhism

"The foolish man conceives the idea of 'self.' The wise man sees there is no ground on which to build the idea of 'self'; thus, he has a right conception of the world and well concludes that all compounds amassed by sorrow will be dissolved again, but the truth will remain."

~ Buddha

It is widely held that Taoism's origins stretch back to the 4th century BCE – if not earlier – drawing from one of the oldest Chinese texts, the I Ching. This text is estimated to have been written around 2500 years ago by the Zhou people. Taoism was also inspired in its early days by the cosmology of the School of Yin-Yang, also known as the School of Naturalists.

It is widely believed that the old master Lao Tzu produced the Taoist philosophy. Legend has it that he sprang from the womb fully gray-haired and brimming with wisdom (around 604 BCE). After taking a position as head librarian of the imperial archives, he became disillusioned by society's ways and left his home to live the rest of his life in quiet solitude. Departing for the final time after a return visit to the city, the gatekeeper asked him to write his parting thoughts, later referred to as the Tao Te Ching, the central text of Taoism.

Taoism is a religious and philosophical tradition based on individuals achieving harmony with the *Tao* (the Way). The Tao is an undefinable, unknowable force that describes ultimate reality; it is the complete makeup of all existence, permeating everything while also being the origin of everything. It explains the power that drives the universe as well as human nature. The Tao teaches that everything is one despite appearances to the contrary. Lao Tzu would have been a contemporary of Confucius (b. 551 BCE). They were both influential philosophers of dynastic China whose influence continues to reverberate throughout the world today.

Confucius, at first a political advisor to rulers of the Chou dynasty, later left to teach groups of students. He stressed upright conduct and human virtue which stems from Jen, an all-encompassing, undefinable force much like the Tao. Confucianism included many ritual ceremonies and instructions for a variety of social conventions, but also contains the more popular, wise, sometimes witty sayings recorded by his students, known as the analects. So influential were these sayings that they remained the predominant social philosophy of China right up until the rule of the last emperor in 1911.

Taoism, unlike Confucianism, does not contain the more rigid rituals and social order characteristic of the latter tradition. Taoist ethics often focus on *wu wei* (action without intention), involving naturalness, simplicity and spontaneity, and accompanied by the "Three Treasures" of compassion, frugality and humility. It is hard to define Taoism because it emphasizes that underlying essence of reality which is undefinable. Leaning into the undefinable and contradictory natures of life, though, is key to Taoist practices. Through recognizing these natures in our own selves, and accepting them as they exist in us, is how to achieve harmony with the universe.

Hinduism is one of the oldest known organized religions with sacred writings dating as far back as 1500 BCE, arising primarily in the region of India. It has various religious schools of thought, some more pantheistic than others (Brahmanism), more panentheistic (Ramanuja), monistic (Sankara), and theistic (Bhakti). Schools of thoughts can be so varied to even include atheism, nihilism and deism. What ties them together are the ancient texts known as the Vedas and the belief that actions have consequences in this life and the next (karma and reincarnation). In ancient Sanskrit texts Brahma is a creator god, and originator of the four Vedas (ancient literature and religious texts).

There is a misconception that Hindus are strictly polytheistic, worshiping many equal gods, or that Hinduism is only pantheistic, believing God is the natural universe and nothing more. Hindus by and large believe in one all-encompassing God giving rise to the entire universe (there are minority exceptions). But it is not strictly a theist belief that God is above the world or completely separate. Rather it is a form of panentheism which finds God both in the world and above it.

Historically there are four primary Hindu denominations which know the supreme God by one name. It is true that there are a wide variety of gods or statues one can worship, such as the popular elephant god Ganesh (son of Shiva) as well as countless other local village gods or goddesses. However, most Hindus see the vast multitude of Hindu gods as metaphorical representations of the one God. Others see a pantheon of lower gods (such as the divas) as heavenly beings that go through lifetimes like other beings, such as people and animals. And yet others still believe all that the universe contains emanates from God alone who splits into many parts, of which our personal experience is but a mere game that God is playing.

Westerners are sometimes accused, rightfully so, of being orientalists when taking account of Eastern history, culture, philosophy, and cosmology. We typically find an attitude of superiority in the Western culture. The origins of this superiority are varied, but some of it stems from Westerners' rather recent and successful arrival to advanced technologies, coupled with a strain of Darwinian evolution commonly referred to as "survival of the fittest." That notwithstanding, there are still advantages to having a Western introduction to unfamiliar cultures, religions, and philosophies.

Huston Smith, for instance, has tried to synthesize the whole of Hinduism literature, rituals, art, folkways into a single affirmation, and that is: "You can have what you want."[109] And according to Smith, Indians have come to understand four things that people want. They are pleasure, success, renunciation, and duty. Hindus are seen as being ascetic and life denying. This is misleading, as Hindus do not forbid seeking pleasure or success (as long as you do so with prudence) but rather are encouraged to seek them so long as that is what we truly want. Seeking pleasure and success are the beginning of a path of development. If you want pleasure and wealth, seek them intelligently: "Only the stupid will lie, steal, or cheat for immediate profit, or succumb to addictions."[110]

Renunciation and duty inevitably follow pleasure and success as the repeated pleasures become routine and the drive for success insatiable. One eventually comes to realize that pleasure is not all one wants. It is not that pleasure is bad, it is because "it is too trivial to satisfy one's total nature. Pleasure is essentially private, and the self is too small an object for perpetual enthusiasm."[111]

Some do not always come to this conclusion, though, and one wonders why some can engage in partying, sexual abandonment, accumulation of wealth at any costs, and only want more. It has to be understood in the context of reincarnation and the self spanning multiple lifetimes. Some are swept up "in the flush of novelty, whereas the others, having played the game over and over again, seek other worlds to conquer."[112] Eventually, though, neither the pursuit nor the attainment provides sustainable happiness.

Once one realizes the self that one has been striving so hard to serve is too small, one begins to renounce the ego and turn outwardly to serving others. This, according to Smith, "marks the first great step in religion," which is "the religion of duty." Duty provides many rewards. One can obtain greater happiness by serving countless others instead of only oneself. It brings respect and gratitude from your peers and self-respect. But just as the allures of self-seeking pleasure and wealth lose their luster, so too does the constant pursuit of serving others. "For even when time turns community into history, history, standing alone, is finite and hence ultimately tragic. It is tragic not only because it must end – eventually history, too, will die – but in its refusal to be perfected. Hope and history are always light-years apart."[113]

Pleasure, success, and duty are too superficial for what we really want, which lies deeper. These pursuits are only paths to that realization. What we really want is being, knowledge, and joy, and we want these things in infinite abundance.

According to Hindu thought, these things are not only in our reach, but each and every one of us already possess them. "Underlying the human self and animating it is a reservoir of being that never dies, is never exhausted, and is unrestricted in consciousness and bliss. This infinite center of every life, this hidden self or *Atman*, is no less than *Brahman*, the Godhead."[114]

But if this godlike center, this eternal bliss, is in and animating all of us, why do we not feel it in ourselves or see it in others? It is because the eternal universal is buried in the here and now and the facade of self. Smith uses a wonderful analogy to illustrate the point: "A lamp can be covered with dust and dirt to the point of obscuring its light completely. The problem life poses for the human self is to cleanse the dross of its being to the point where its infinite center can shine forth in full display."[115]

Dharma is a central doctrine in Indian philosophy and religion. Its meaning has evolved, just as Hinduism has evolved and has special relevance as applied in Buddhism and Jainism. In the earliest texts, dharma meant cosmic law, but in common practice it means the right way of living or method. Buddhism is therefore a way, method or discipline of Buddha. And a Buddha is a person who is awake. Samsara is the cycle of birth and death from lower life forms to more progressive life forms. Among these life forms you have those that are smart and dumb, seeking and satisfied, but as you progress your way to the top (as a diva for instance) you have nowhere to go but down. Samsara is a result of the illusion that a person is a separate self instead of understanding the connection between the self and all of reality. A Buddha is one who discovers or awakens from this illusion of endless cycle, hence the word "awakened." It is an abandonment of pursuing time, and instead experiencing the now in its total glory.

Out of the ancient Hindu religion Jainism, Buddhism (circa 500 BCE) and Sikhism (around 1500 CE) arose, and in turn were exported. Jainism arose out of reaction to orthodox Brahman Hinduism, and Buddhism arose as a result of the awakening of prince Siddhartha. What their followers are trying to discard is the cycle of rebirth and reincarnation so prominent in Hindu culture. For Jainism this is accomplished through the self-discipline of cleansing one's soul, and principles of nonviolence, non-attachment, and meditation. For Buddhists it is also accomplished by renunciation and meditation, but also by understanding the four noble truths and the eightfold path to enlightenment. Ironically for many Westerners newly enamored with Eastern religion, they are adopting an acceptance of reincarnation for which all serious practitioners of Jainism and Buddhism are trying to liberate themselves from.

To understand Buddhism, it is first essential to understand its founder Prince Siddhartha Gautama, born of King Suddhodana and Queen Maya in the plains region of modern Nepal and India. He had wealth, silver, elephants, a beautiful wife and son, and was set to inherit the throne. But from a very young age he was concerned about the suffering of humanity and its endless repetition through rebirth and reincarnation. Fortune tellers found the young prince to be no ordinary child, predicting he would be a great and universal King and conqueror or, if he chose to forsake the world, a world redeemer. Tradition has it that at 29 years of age he gave up his pampered life, kissed his wife and son goodbye, and set out alone on a quest to find an end to the endless suffering. He first studied for 6 years under accomplished Vedic teachers learning meditation and ancient wisdom, focusing on nothingness and what is neither seen nor unseen. Unsatisfied, he turned to strict asceticism. So strict was the regimen he ate only 6 grains of rice a day, eventually remarking he could practically grab his spine when he touched his stomach, nearly dying from starvation.

Having not found enlightenment through indulgence or strict asceticism, Gautama sought a middle way, adopting rigorous thought and mystic, transic concentration. He famously sat down under the Bo tree, or immovable spot, and vowed to remain until enlightenment was obtained. He was tempted by evil spirits with worldly desires and, when that did not work, by the threat of death and ruin. But Gautama, by emptying his finite self, left no chance for the evil ones to threaten or seduce. The Bo tree rained red blossoms as Gautama became transformed into the Buddha, fully awakened, seeing that he was not separate from the world but merely a facet of the world. Mara, the evil one, tempted him one last time with reason. Why not abandon your body, which is transitory, and give yourself up to nirvana? How will you ever be able to teach that which can only be discovered, speak to that which is unspeakable and undefinable? In this, Gautama Buddha was nearly tempted, but alas he resigned himself to trudging along "the dusty paths of India until his hair was white, step infirm, and body nothing but a burst drum, preaching his ego-shattering, life-redeeming message."[116] At the age of eighty years old he died of dysentery, caused apparently by some dried boar he ate. Part of his final message was, "All compounded things decay. Work out your own salvation with diligence."[117]

Buddha taught us the four noble truths are as follows. We crave and cling to impermanent things, which are incapable of satisfying and painful, and keep us caught in an endless cycle of birth and rebirth, but one may be liberated from the endless cycle to a state of nirvana (by following the eightfold path). For Buddhists nirvana is realization of non-self, whereas in Hindu philosophy it is the union of the inner self (Atman) with the transcendent, all-encompassing self or ultimate reality and cause of all that exists (Brahman). The eightfold path consists of developing the right path, right view, intention, speech, action, livelihood, effort, mindfulness and concentration. The latter of which is achieved through the correct meditation.

Alan Watts, a popular British philosopher who relocated to San Francisco, introduced Eastern philosophy to a Western audience in a unique and authentic style. He wrote a number of essays and books and hosted numerous lectures on various subjects, including Zen Buddhism, in the 60s and 70s. His talks and essays helped synthesize the spirit and goals of Buddhism in a way that was relatable to his English-speaking audience.

Watts described all of reality as consisting of being and non-being propagated in waves or vibrations. He reminds us that as a species we have developed specialization in concentrated attention. But the price we pay for specialized attention is ignorance of everything outside its field. "Our physical world," he says, "is a system of inseparable difference. Everything exists with everything else. We contrive not to notice that. Because what we notice is what is noteworthy." You cannot describe the behavior of an organism without describing the environment of which it is in. But the "organism is not the puppet of the environment nor on the other hand is the environment the puppet of the organism." They are part of a unified field of behavior which is roughly what every mystic would conclude. That is, one's awareness "of his inseparability as an individual from the total existing universe."

Each one of us is an organism with a central nervous system of which we couldn't begin to describe in totality how it works. When we breathe and digest, are we aware of our digesting and breathing? Instead of thinking of us doing the breathing, we should look at the universe breathing through us. We tend to delineate things that are fuzzy to find lines where there are curves. The idea of God as the handicrafter gives you meaning. "But after a while it becomes embarrassing," says Watts, "so you become an atheist. But you feel bad when you get rid of God because then you are just a machine devoid of meaning. This gives rise to the automatic mechanical theory of the universe which says I will impose my will upon the universe." These are the prickly people, as Watts describes, who are exacting and precise – logical positivists – as opposed to the goo people who like things vague – the idealists. But you can't have one without the other. "This whole idea that the universe is just nothing at all but unintelligent force playing around and not even enjoying it," says Watts, "is a put down theory of the world."[118]

The quintessence of all of Watts' teaching and object of all Buddhist training is, in Watts' own words, "to bring about a state of affairs in which an individual feels himself to be everything there is, the whole cosmos, focused, expressing itself here." And in that way, you would not forget who you are or your role in society but would understand that this role, this personality, "is superficial and the real you is all that there is. And that inversion, turning upside down the sense of identity, the state of consciousness that the average person has is the objective of Buddhistic discipline." The satori, or experience of awakening, is when "you discover that what you are is no longer this sort of isolated center of action and experience locked up in your skin… [I]t isn't there and when you see clearly that it isn't there, you have a new sense of identity and when you realize that, what you are is, as I said, the whole world of nature doing this. You then see that you are what the entire cosmos is doing at this place."[119]

Allan Watts' cosmology is a blend of modern physics with ancient Hindu philosophy and Zen Buddhism. However, it is purely pantheistic (all is god). And, like the mechanical automatic view of the world he criticizes, it has trouble providing meaning. In Watts' cosmology, reality is seen as a play or dance or music without any more meaning than we ascribe to it, to only be enjoyed now for what it is. Philosophy and religions are offered to give life meaning or purpose. The kind of pantheism Watts espouses does not require additional meaning. If we want to feel that all things have significance, we have to look at them in a certain way. Significance is a quality of a state of mind. "The significance in the world seems to be the world what is going on now and we don't look any further." What you are left with then in such a worldview is the license to do whatever you want to do (or choose to get out of the cyclical game altogether), as opposed to what you ought to do.

Most Hindus and Buddhists, of which Watts can be included, do not believe in God in the traditional sense. On the one hand they readily accept and ascribe to a nature of reality consisting of a power or creative force that permeates the universe (of which we are part of). This view, although ancient, is not entirely inconsistent with our modern understanding of the way the world really works. But can it be reconciled with Western religion? Is God separate from the world? Is God everything and everything God? Is God both in the world and above it? Or is God an outdated notion, as the modern atheists suppose, and all reality mechanical, material, and automatic?

-B-

THE CURRENT SCIENCE PERSPECTIVE

8

Science's Creation Story: a universe with and without substance

"For after all what is man in nature? ... The ends of things and their beginnings are impregnably concealed from him in an impenetrable secret. He is equally incapable of seeing the nothingness out of which he was drawn and the infinite in which he is engulfed."

~ Blaise Pascal, Pensées No. 72

Science gives us a model of reality and the universe on the smallest scales and on the largest, with theories for everything in between. It gives an account for the beginnings of the universe and the formation of simpler and heavier elements, along with evolving planetary systems and eventually life. Whether life exists outside of our planet we do not yet have definitive proof, but statistically it is agreed it is highly probable. Our understanding of what nature is made of, including its microscopic properties and cosmological properties, is advanced but still incomplete.

Both ancient Greece and India developed atomism as a natural philosophy in which they thought nature consisted of atoms –

primary indestructible units of substance – and the void in which the atoms collide and interact with each other form the macroscopic substances in the world we experience. Modern physics has proved this theory but has found that the atoms are made of electrons, protons, and neutrons, and they in turn are made of quarks, which are the only elementary particles in today's model of physics. Further, quantum field theory tells us that everywhere in the universe is an electron field and that every electron is nothing more than a localized vibration in that whole field (just as every particle has its own unique field).[120] Particle accelerators slam particles together so we can witness vibrations in these fields. At the most fundamental levels of nature we understand that material substance is an illusion created by multiple, infinitely large vibrations.

Substance, and other than substance, is everywhere according to current models of physics and science. One can still say that all tangible things are comprised of substance, but not that all of reality and the entire universe is made of things or substance or material. You could, but you would have to concede that the vast void of nothing we recognize at micro and macro scales could contain something(s) but we have yet to detect or identify what that or those something(s) are (at least at the cosmic levels of deep space and levels smaller than quarks).

Subatomic particles (such as photons) act as both waves and particles. Mechanical and electromagnetic waves are the way energy is transported throughout the universe. The matter that waves travel through is called a medium, which causes molecules to bump into each other creating a domino effect. Water waves act by vibrations through liquid, and sound waves by vibrations in gas or air. Mechanical waves, like sound, cannot travel through the vacuum of space (because there are no molecules). Outer space is the closest thing we have to a perfect vacuum with virtually no friction. It is nearly devoid of visible matter containing only a few hydrogen atoms per cubic meter.

Electromagnetic waves, on the other hand, do not need a medium to propagate. They can travel through air and solid material as well as the vacuum of space. A radio wave is a wave of electromagnetic frequency of about ten to the fourth hertz (waves per second). The velocity of radio waves is equal to the velocity of light. Radio waves travel from a transmitter to a receiver in which the electrons inside it vibrate, recreating the original signal. Through a device called a radio, millions of people can pick up a coded radio signal from a single powerful transmitter. Encoding of information is accomplished by varying the frequency of the wave or the signal strength of the wave.

Light is just one form of electromagnetic radiation. Some we can see with our eyes and others we cannot. The further you move from the source, the greater diminishment in the intensity of the radiation. In some ways it displays wave phenomenon; in other respects it acts like a high-speed submicroscopic particle. Once created, an electromagnetic wave will continue on forever unless it is absorbed by matter. The smallest (4x10^9 inches) of electromagnetic waves with the highest frequency we can detect are gamma rays.[121] The longest on the spectrum (0.4 inch) have the lowest frequency.[122]

That is not to say that there can be no other longer or shorter waves that are not currently detectable. It is also possible, even likely, that other waves exist and are present but not mechanical in the traditional sense, or electromagnetic, but just have not as yet been discovered. Waves, though, are the predominant force and structure present throughout the universe and have helped in creating its structure.

The currently accepted model of the formation of the universe describes the very early universe as forming the first fundamental forces such as gravity and electromagnetism, along with expansion and super cooling of an extremely, almost infinitely dense and hot mass 13.8 billion years ago.[123] At only a few minutes after the beginning of the Big Bang (a massive explosion like event that caused a rapid expansion of the early universe) conditions were no longer hot enough for fusion, but hot enough to prevent photons from traveling and was therefore a dark, opaque plasma.

Almost 400,000 years after the beginning, the universe became cool enough to be transparent and for atoms to form and reach their lowest energy state by releasing photons, which can still be observed today as the cosmic microwave background. This marked the appearance of the first light in the universe. Shortly thereafter clouds of hydrogen began to collapse very slowly to form the earliest stars and galaxies. These early stars burned their hydrogen fuel quickly and exploded into supernovae.

About 10 million years after the Big Bang, the average temperature of the universe was around 100 Celsius, or the boiling point of water. At about 17 million years after the beginning, the universe had expanded and cooled to the freezing point of water or 0 Celsius. Some astronomers therefore theorize that the entire universe contained liquid water for around 7 million years, possibly even suitable for a brief time to support life under the right conditions.[124]

From a billion years after the Big Bang (or 12.8 billion years ago), the universe has looked pretty much the same as it has today and is predicted it will for billions of years to come as it continues to expand, absent some cosmic apocalyptic event. The thin disk of our galaxy began to form about 9 billion years ago, our solar system about 4.6 billion years ago, and life on earth around 3.8 billion years ago.

These estimates, based on observations of background radiation and fossil rocks as well as astronomical observations, are not always precise. Particularly with the four-billion-year difference between the formation of our Milky Way galaxy and that of our solar system. Since galaxy, star, and planet forming is a slow accumulative process, these calculations are estimates. In other words, at what point do you call a galaxy filled with millions of stars a galaxy, or an accumulation of rock, dust and debris a planet?

The heavier elements which make up the planets did not form until after being run through the nuclear reaction of stars after successive populations of supernova explosions in the vicinity of our Milky Way galaxy. It was only in the last 5 to ten billion years that Population I stars, like our sun, began to produce and broadcast their heavier elements that fed the material that makes up our solar system, including earth.[125]

In the time it took to form the universe as we know it today, about one third consisted in forming the first stars and galaxies, and two thirds to form the beginning of our Milky Way galaxy, sun, earth and moon sufficiently to sustain life here on earth. This makes our place in the universe very unique but not necessarily central. Since we observe galaxies moving away from us in all directions at increasing speed, it is possible to theorize it's because we are at the center of the Big Bang. However, most accept that we are not at the center of the Big Bang and have other theories to explain why the universe is expanding uniformly in the way it appears to be.

Gravity is the force in the universe that pulls matter together. In areas of the early universe where it was denser, it naturally drew more mass and material together and formed our currently existing galaxies. The problem though is, based on our current observation of visible matter in galaxies and the clusters they are a part of, there is much less mass present to account for their being held together and not flying apart. To make up for this difficult-to-explain observation, physicists have proposed a theoretical type of invisible matter dubbed dark matter. To correct for the error, it is estimated 27% of the matter throughout the universe and within galaxies is made of such theoretical matter.[126]

As for the expansion of the universe as a whole, it is expanding at a much faster rate than either observable or dark matter can answer for. To account for this, theorists have proposed that there is also a hidden, undetectable, repulsive force dubbed dark energy. It is estimated that this energy makes up 68% of the matter throughout the universe and is thought to explain the universe's unexpected expansion.[127] So, on the one hand there is a theoretical explanation for why things in the universe – such as galaxies and galaxy clusters – are staying together when they should not, and another to explain why as a whole they are flying away from each other when, again, they should not, at least not at the rate we observe. Of course, there are alternative theories to explain this anomaly as well.

The Big Wave theory proposes that the Big Bang would produce waves outwards from the center, but that it is possible to have smaller waves throughout that would send galaxies rippling outward from such new centers. Since we observe galaxies moving away from us in all directions at increasing speed, it is possible to theorize it's because we are at the center of an expansion wave or even much more improbably at the center of the Big Bang. But for us to be at the center (of the Big Bang or a sizable expansion wave) would be quite coincidental.

According to standard physics models, the Big Bang would have created equal amounts of matter and anti-matter, but the visible universe appears to be dominated by structures made up of the common matter we are familiar with. Where is all the anti-matter? Some suggest it is spread throughout the universe in large-scale voids empty of visible stars and galaxies. These voids could be made up of enormous superstructures complete with galaxies, solar systems and planets of their own but are not emitting radiation that we can detect. Because matter and antimatter repel each other, it could explain the observable expansion of the universe without relying on dark energy as its cause.

A third, less popular alternative theory is that of an electric universe. 99.999% of the visible universe is a plasma and all plasmas produce their own magnetic field and electric currents. Currents flow through extragalactic jets covering multiple parsecs (vast distances in space). Within our own solar system and galaxy there is a constant flow of current between 30 to the 9th power and 10 to the 17th power. Interacting electric currents applied to plasmas produce spiral formations characteristic of large-scale galaxies. Because plasmas are shaped by electromagnetic forces, electric universe theorists suggest that the universe's structures are better explained by electromagnetic properties than black holes, dark matter, dark energy and the Big Bang.[128]

Even though it's possible life may have started on earth in more than one place, the theory of evolution generally holds that all species are related, stem from a common ancestor, and gradually changed over time. In 1859 Charles Darwin described in *On the Origin of Species* how living organisms "evolve" over successive generations through the inheritance of physical or behavioral traits. Individuals within a species that have certain traits that make them better adapted to their environment will have a better chance at surviving and passing on those favorable traits to their offspring.

Although Darwin did not completely understand it at the time, the mechanism for the evolution of species occurs at the genome level. DNA is the molecular hereditary material in humans that contains the biological instructions that make each species unique. It contains all the information necessary to build and maintain an organism and its successive offspring. Changes in these instruction sequences happen due to environmental exposures and random chance events known as mutations. When these mutations occur the traits of the organism can change significantly over successive generations. For example, we as humans share about 40% of our DNA with bananas, about 60% with fruit flies, and about 98.6% with chimpanzees.

Our earth was fully formed around 4.8 billion years ago. The first life form emerged shortly thereafter between 4.3 and 3.7 billion years ago in some sort of primordial soup. Those earliest life forms were asexually reproducing, metabolizing microorganisms and living rock-like structures called stromatolites. Whether that first soup was in a bubbling cauldron of mud and water on land or a mineral-rich hydrothermal vent under the ocean is still being determined.[129] About a billion years ago the first sexually reproducing organisms appeared, and at about half a billion years ago the first fish and land plants as well. Dinosaurs evolved from earlier reptiles about 250 million years ago, going extinct in part as the result of an enormous asteroid strike 66 million years ago in the Yucatán Peninsula.

Mammals, which appear shortly after the dinosaurs, evolved into various species including the great apes and monkeys. Genetic studies indicate the split between humans and chimpanzees occurred about 6 million years ago, which also coincided with walking upright instead of strictly on all fours. The most prolific of these ape-like man species is Australopithecus. They were widespread until their extinction about 2 million years ago, which coincided with the rise and proliferation of early human species such as *Homo habilis* and *Homo erectus*. *Homo erectus* was larger, and had a slightly bigger brain, than *Australopithecus*, and could make fires and use stone tools. In turn Neanderthals and *Homo sapiens* had bigger brains than either *Homo erectus* or *Australopithecus* (roughly 3 times as large a cranial capacity).[130] Some of these early hominid species lived in close proximity to one another, even occasionally interbreeding (such as between us, *Homo sapiens*, and Neanderthals).

The earliest remains of any direct human relative date to 430,000 years ago found at the bottom of a cave in Spain known as Sima de los Huesos, the "Pit of Bones." The DNA extracted from the bones and teeth that were discovered revealed they belong to the oldest known Neanderthals, one of our closest human relatives.

By analyzing the genetic material, scientists were, with the aid of a theoretical genetic molecular clock, able to calculate approximately how long it took to accumulate the differences between these earliest discovered Neanderthals and modern humans. Armed with this information they were able to calculate that a common ancestor of the two lived sometime approximately 700,000 years ago.[131]

From uncovering the ancient remains of our human relatives to deciphering the genetic paths of evolution, science has grounded our existence in the tangible, deterministic world of matter. Yet, as we delve into the mysteries of subatomic particles, we encounter a paradigm shift, leaving behind the solidity of the macroscopic for a realm of unpredictability and probabilities. This transition bridges our cosmological understanding of causal predictability to a world of randomness where particles exist more as waves than as substance, challenging our perceptions of reality and the underpinnings of our existence.

With the advent of wave and energy mechanics, modern physics is moving away from a strictly deterministic universe to one "of pure randomness where a particle can appear anywhere in space and time according to probabilities dictated by quantum mechanics."[132] For such a particle to appear anywhere at any time would be quite unpredictable and chaotic. However, on the Planck scale (the bottom layer of existence), the universe's movements are binary, where one frame only interacts with the adjoining frame apparently following strict deterministic rules of yes or no answers, this or that possibility.[133]

In other words, at a macroscopic level the motions of galaxies, stars, and objects like ourselves are dictated by the laws of cause and effect, but on a subatomic quantum level nothing is determined until you look at it. This stems from what is known as the uncertainty principle or observer effect.[134] At this level the very act of choosing to observe a thing changes that thing. It appears then as though consciousness itself (or at least an entity's interaction with other entities) may be necessary to reduce the superposition of possible states of matter (such as wave or particle). Although this sounds counterintuitive, it is a well-documented physics phenomenon. At some basic rudimentary level, science accepts immaterial forces are at work that preface and order our "material" world. The irony being that in so doing they are also, in some sense, becoming more spiritual in their outlook (whereby spirituality is embracing an ultimate immaterial reality).

Keep in mind that everything in the universe is made of matter except energy. Matter is the stuff in the universe that has mass and takes up space, while energy is the capacity to cause change. Atoms (small units of matter), are made up of spinning vortices of energy constantly vibrating like a tiny, invisible top radiating its own energy. Light is an example of such energy. It is at the intersection of matter and energy, behaving both like a particle and a wave. We are told energy cannot be created or destroyed, but only converted from one form to another and thus believe energy is more primary than matter. However, there are yet others who say information is more primary than either matter or energy. Theorist Paul Davies calls it the "'ontological basement' of reality."[135]

Reality, or what we consider real, consists of everything there is and everything we can do and perceive. It also consists of everything we can see or imagine. But what we see and what we imagine are two different aspects of reality. Just because we can conceive of something does not make it an external reality, even though the conception itself is real.

Perceptions are drawn from sources outside ourselves, while conceptions and imagination are created from sources within ourselves. Bear in mind perceptions and conceptions are integrated. Just because we are conceiving something in our minds at a locale we roughly call our center, it is still a phenomenon that is happening in space and time and every bit a part of reality, even taking place within physical reality. But the conception itself is a construct built from the various perceptions we have experienced through our sensory apparatus. It is for this reason there has been historically some confusion about separating mind and body, consciousness from substance. For example, the French philosopher René Descartes formally declared the mind and the brain two separate but related things.[136] The distinction is more one of energy versus matter.

Scientists taking a strictly materialist view propose that knowing the fundamental laws of nature precludes the possibility of life after death. Because there is no way for the soul (or consciousness) to survive the body and there is no way for the information you have acquired to be carried outside your body and to be compiled and transferred to some other organism or receptacle at some other time. Presumably there are no particles or interactions that could allow this to happen.

However, breakthroughs in modern science show that the brain transmits information through electrochemical signals that link together different regions of information through neuronal oscillations. But oscillating electrical signals are more like energy than what we formally call substance. We cannot say consciousness is made up of substance any more than we can say vibrations and energy are made of matter. But matter and energy, even information, are a part of reality – are a part of nature.

Physics has come to show us that all particles or groups of particles exist also as waves, and waves exist in multiple places at the same time. Thus, theoretically any collection of matter can occupy two places at the same time. Considering electrons are part of an infinite, non-localized field, coupled with the fact that electrons can occupy two points at the same time – actually an infinite number of points – then you have a non-localized substrate for consciousness that can manifest in a localized receptor.

It is becoming clear that there is something in consciousness that is fundamentally different from all other things in the physical world. Advances in physics and quantum mechanics are showing how entangled pairs of subatomic matter may communicate in and across the void of the brain instantly. And theoretically to continue communicating even if the brain were to malfunction or die so long as the subatomic particles comprising the consciousness and memories remain entangled.

Physicists also tell us at the microscopic level there is no purpose or teleological goal. For example, professor Carroll concedes that at the macroscopic level there could be purpose but not at the microscopic or quantum level.[137] Similarly, Darwin says there is no contradiction in saying evolution has no purpose but organisms have purpose. Just as most scientists and atheists do not believe nature will provide us purpose, they also believe science will not provide answers as to what is right and wrong. As alluded to earlier, some have come up with objective, rational-based models for morals, but in the end, despite their best efforts, they are highly subjective and not necessarily absolute or universal. It then comes down to whether man is the measure of all things. It also comes down to whether man can measure all things.

Is there a limit to what we can know? To what we can detect? To whether we can answer the question of whether a supreme being exists? Are we constrained by what we can know, or is what we can know and detect limitless? The answer is no, we (individually in our current configuration) cannot know everything, but we can focus on some aspects of everything, and we can conceptualize everything. Whether we can detect everything is a harder question to answer. We cannot – with our limited expected life span and sensory perceptions, and even with a plethora of sensory expanding tools – possibly detect everything there is to be detected. But given enough time and tools, could we? The answer is still no. The only concept of a being that can know and detect everything that ever was or ever could be known and detected is that of a supreme being. And one thing we can probably all concede to, is that we (at least individually) are not supreme beings.

One could imagine sentient beings evolving to a high degree of awareness, capacity for knowledge, and omniscience, but it is hard to imagine total omniscience. And even if countless such beings could be truly omniscient, it is harder to imagine them all being omnipotent; otherwise, assuming such beings of free will, they would necessarily limit the power of the others unless they all had a singular will and purpose. Then you would have a situation where, out of many, you have one. If only one such being could somehow evolve, you are still faced with the fact that such being evolved in a universe that was already created and thus would not be truly omnipotent (for having relied on other than itself, himself, and herself for its existence). Only a single omniscient source can know everything. That source is the foundation of monotheism.

-C-

THE MIDDLE EASTERN AND WESTERN PERSPECTIVE

9

Judaism

"...[T]here is but one religion under many forms, whose essential creed is the Fatherhood of God, and the Brotherhood of Man,—disguised by corruptions, symbolized by mythologies, ennobled by virtues, degraded by vices, but still the same."

~ Thomas Wentworth Higginson, February 6th 1870

"Tell Joseph to go and find his grief-stricken father, Jacob. Blinded by the blood-stained shirt and his disappearance, Joseph's triumphs in Egypt are Jacob's tribulations."

~ Rumi, 1207-1273

Judaism, Christianity, and Islam are all part of the same Abrahamic religion that recognizes and glorifies God as the creator of the universe and all its creatures. They all understand mankind was created with apprehension and reason sufficient to choose between right and wrong, and will be rewarded for the good we do whether in this life or the hereafter. They all believe God has provided mankind with revelatory moral insights and laws to help make themselves and society better.

It is important, though, to differentiate between the revelatory messages and their commentaries. Commentaries may offer insight and shape practice, but they do not carry the same weight as the original messages they explain or expand upon. Additionally, what is accepted as core tenets or scripture of each faith may not necessarily be authentic or historically accurate. Nonetheless, the stories they tell are undoubtedly based on actual events, if not necessarily from firsthand accounts.

There are common patterns of monotheism arising in the midst of polytheistic belief systems. Examples include the Aten (a manifestation of the sun god Ra) cult in ancient Egypt and the rise in prominence of Yahweh from a divine warrior to God of the entire world in the ancient kingdom of Israel. The word "Hebrew" is believed to come from the ancient term Habiru, loosely describing the multitude of then-wandering outcasts from the Nile to the Euphrates river. The Habiru, who worshiped the god Horus, were called Horites and were of a caste of ruler priests who considered the sun an emblem of the creator, practiced circumcision, and sacrificed animals at an altar.

Ancient hieroglyphs unearthed in Egypt mention Sechem being given to the Habiru. The land of Sechem, in upper Galilee, is where the biblical prophet Abraham is said to have first set foot in Canaan (modern-day Israel and Palestine). The first recorded reference to Israel is found in a monument erected in 1207 BCE by the Egyptian Pharaoh Meneptah to commemorate his victory over the Canaanites, which states "Israel is wasted but its seed is not."

Judaism (from the tribe of Judah) – along with Zoroastrianism – is amongst the first recorded monotheistic religions, with the Torah, consisting of the five books of Moses (the Pentateuch), making up its foundational text. According to the central text of Rabbinic Judaism, most of the Hebrew bible was completed in 450 BCE. This was shortly after the fall of Babylon at the hands of Cyrus (sometimes referred to as Cyrus the Great) and the return of the Israelites to Jerusalem starting in 539 BCE.

The main tenets of Judaism include belief in one omnipotent God who created the universe, praying to God alone, and following his commandments (which include a number of rules and rituals) which were revealed to his prophets, including Moses at Mount Sinai. Unlike the sometimes fickle and unpredictable gods portrayed in Greek and Roman mythology, God for the Jewish people was seen as just and fair.

In Judaism, God is both transcendent and personal but is not a person. Rather God has personal attributes and emotions, and can form relationships with peoples and nations. In the Hebrew bible we find a God who hears and answers and "portrays an encounter with a God who cares passionately and who addresses humanity in the quiet moments of its existence." And as British chief Rabbi Jonathan Sacks explains, God "is not distant in time or detached, but passionately engaged and present."[138]

There are various Jewish religious groups whose main differences are their interpretation of the religious laws. According to Orthodox Judaism these moral laws are divine, eternal, unalterable and require strict adherence; whereas Reform Judaism sees these laws more as general guidelines rather than strict rules. The most important and central of these legal and moral laws are those revealed by God to his prophet Moses in the form of a written and Oral Torah, including the Ten Commandments. We find in Judaism God entering into a number of agreements or covenants with man, starting with a promise of paradise and eternal life to Adam on condition of not eating from the tree of moral knowledge (Gen. 2:15), through a promise to Jeremiah of a new covenant to come in which God will put his law in his people's hearts (Jeremiah 31:31-33).

Genesis, the first book of the Old Testament, narrates the cosmological and ancestral history of humanity, beginning with Adam, the first man. It details the struggles and triumphs of various peoples, with particular focus on the prophets, their messages, and examples. Ten generations after Adam, Prophet Noah appears who, along with a few faithful followers, was saved from an all-encompassing flood. Nine generations after Noah's son Shem, we meet Abraham, a common patriarch in Judaism, Christianity, and Islam. He establishes an agreement, or covenant, of God's blessings in return for his and his descendants' devotion and faithfulness. Abraham had two sons, Isaac and Ishmael, with his wife Sarah and Egyptian wife Hagar, respectively. Isaac's son Jacob had 12 sons, including Joseph.

According to Genesis 37, Joseph had a dream that while he and his 11 brothers were making bundles of wheat his bundle stood up and their bundles bowed down to his, as did the sun, the moon and eleven stars. This made the brothers jealous, so they one day threw him in a deep well and kept his coat which they smeared goat's blood on. They then gave the coat (in the Quran, it is a shirt) to Jacob to lead him to believe he was eaten by a wild animal. In response, Jacob vowed to go to his grave mourning his son.

Joseph later made his way to Egypt, gained prominent status, predicted and prepared for a seven-year drought, and eventually forgave his brothers.[139] And to his father's relief, Joseph revealed he was still alive and invited Jacob and his family to stay and settle with him in Egypt.[140] These Hebrew transplants eventually fell out of favor with the Egyptians who subjugated them until they were finally freed and led out of Egypt by Moses with the miraculous parting of the Red Sea (Sea of Reeds) back into the land of Canaan around 1500 to 1200 BCE. Jacob's 12 children – including Joseph, Levi and Judah – are famously known as the heads of the 12 tribes of Israel. From Adam to Abraham there were 21 generations according to the Old Testament, and approximately 60-80 generations from Adam to Jesus according to the Old and New Testaments.

These genealogies often include the prophets' and their descendants' ages, such as Adam fathering Seth at 130 years old and living for another 800 years. Since anatomically modern humans have existed for over 10,000 generations, this poses an issue for those taking the genealogies literally, assuming no gaps (especially considering an average estimated human lifespan of not more than 40 years).

Historical records establish that a large number of people from the ancient kingdom of Judah were taken by the Babylonians and held captive approximately 35 miles south of modern Baghdad in 597 BCE. Some have suggested (as Hitchens hints in *God is not Great*) that the detailed ritual and legal admonitions of the Pentateuch (first five books of the Old Testament) only came after the Babylonian captivity and may have even been ordered by the Babylonian authority itself. This is plausible for the compilation but it is well accepted and evidenced by the archaeological record that Hebrew rituals and rules predated 6th century BCE.

The 12th century Rabbi Abraham ibn Ezra was among the first to openly question the Pentateuch, having been written at the time of Moses. The prominent Jewish philosopher Spinoza drew heavily from ibn Ezra's findings and argued that "it is as clear as the noonday light that the Pentateuch was not written by Moses, but by one who lived many ages after him."[141]

Current biblical scholarship agrees that the Pentateuch was not authored verbatim by Moses but is the result of an ongoing literary process that continued until after the Jewish return to Israel after the Babylonian captivity (around 500 years after Moses arrived in Israel).[142] That notwithstanding, it is still considered the most authoritative of the Old Testament texts. In it is recorded a reported speech given by Moses to a local audience on the plains of Moab (in modern-day Jordan), which foreshadows the coming of a future prophet amongst their midst, similar to Moses, for whom God would put His words in his mouth.[143] Some believed this prophet would be from the tribe of Levi, like Moses and his brother Aaron. Others suggest it refers to Jesus or Muhammad. Keep in mind that in both Islam and Judaism, Abraham left Hagar, his Egyptian wife, in the Arabian Peninsula, where she gave birth to Ishmael. And it is commonly understood that both Moses and Muhammad were prophets with a legal as well as spiritual message. Thus it is conceivable that the spiritual blessings of any covenant between Abraham and God would fall upon all of his descendants, both Arabs and Jews.

However, it is more commonly believed that Jesus (himself from the house of Judah) was the bearer of the new covenant: the one who was to place the law in the people's hearts (as a salvation to the house of Israel and Judah) as foretold by Jeremia (31:33), not the future prophet mentioned by Moses. The Levites, mentioned in Genesis for their treacherous attack on Sechem, have since the time of Aaron considered to be the holders of the priesthood.[144] Hathor Meri, the patroness-goddess of ancient Horite metalworkers, some of whom may have included Aaron, is an important figure in this context. Legend has it Meri conceived Horus, the seed of the one God Ra, by the power of the overshadowing sun. Other rulers could be also conceived by such a method but if such rulers did not rise after death, their divinity was disproved. Some see in this myth a Horite-Levite genealogical and spiritual connection to the virgin birth of Mary and her son Jesus rising from the dead, as well as the heavenly-father-earthly-son symbolism.[145]

Whether the prophesized one was meant to be a Levite or not, it is clear from the historical record that the Israelites were awaiting a prophet at the time of Jesus and some believed that Jesus was the prophet that Moses was referring to. Most did not, however, and today many Orthodox Jews continue to await a messiah. However, when considering the foretelling that he was to enter Jerusalem riding a donkey (Zachariah 9:9), to be born of a virgin (Isaiah 7:14), born of the tribe of Judah (Gen 49:10), descended from King David (Isaiah 9:7), as well as other detailed references to a future prophet, it can be argued Jesus' coming was indeed prophesied (even if he was not the prophet foretold on the plains of Moab). Such fulfilled prophecies may provide support for possible divine or superhuman revelation, but at the same time many more prophecies remain unfulfilled.

We tend to think of ideas, values, and beliefs as unique to peoples and places, but in fact they are an ever-changing, ever-evolving conglomeration of exchanged interactions. What people often reserve for themselves is a bounty that all humanity is ready to receive, whether inherited prophetic lineage or rationalistic framework. Yet despite the exchange of ideas and beliefs between cultures throughout history, conflicts and tensions have also arisen between them. One such conflict is illustrated by the Maccabean war during the Hellenistic periods of Greek flourishing. This period saw the spread of a rational and logic-based culture, which was in conflict with the traditional Jewish beliefs and practices.

Aristotle's student Alexander of Macedonia – carefully trained in philosophy, science, and the art of warfare – at around 320 BCE became one of the most successful generals ever known, conquering much of the entire ancient world including Syria, Egypt and Palestine. The conquered lands under his rule were allowed to continue their own particular religious observances and customs. Many of the subject peoples, however, including the Jews, naturally adopted Greek customs, language and dress. But just as important, the Greeks, then Romans, and in turn modern Europeans, have adopted much of what can today be considered the Judeo-Christian (and increasingly Islamic) tradition.

Jennifer Hecht suggests that Jews and Greeks had a friendly relationship. "The Jews who enjoyed Hellenistic culture may not have felt any less Jewish, seeing nothing ill in the Greek invitation to civic celebrations, universalist moral philosophy, exercise and education in the Gymnasium, a sense of progress, and a prosperous future for the kids."[146] But others were not as convinced, as the story of Judah Maccabee effectively illustrates.

Around 168 BCE, during the Hanukkah story, Syria and Egypt were fighting for control of the land of Israel. The Greeks and Syrians were promoting idol worship and a way of life that was becoming increasingly popular among the Israelites. However, during the Hellenistic (ancient Greek culture after Alexander) period, it was considered dangerous to question the gods, which resulted in the execution of many Jews by the Syrian king Antiochus. Jewish worship, including circumcision, Sabbath, and dietary restrictions, were forbidden under penalty of death, with some Jews even being killed for refusing to eat pork.

In response to the harsh penalties, Judah Maccabee's father, a Jewish priest, killed an apostate Hellenistic Jew, sparking the Maccabean war. Antiochus sent 40,000 well-equipped soldiers to wipe out the outnumbered Jewish defenders, but ultimately lost. The Maccabees were able to liberate Jerusalem and found a single jar of oil in the temple, which normally only lasted a day, but miraculously burned for eight days. This event is commemorated today through the menorah lighting customs of Hanukkah.

During this time, the culture of the Hellenistic period was spreading, and many Jews voluntarily adopted Greek rationalism. Following the restoration of the temple, the Hasmonean Dynasty ruled, and there were uncustomary conversions of non-Jews by the sword. However, this rule only lasted for about a century before control was taken over by the Roman client king of Judea, Herod, with the help of Mark Antony. Jerusalem remained under Roman control until 637 CE when the Christian Patriarch Sophronius surrendered the city to Omar ibn al-Khattab, Islam's second caliph.

10
Christianity

"If triangles had a God, He'd have three sides."
~ Old Yiddish Proverb

Most modern accounts of Jesus come from the four Gospels of the Bible: Mark, Matthew, Luke and John. These four gospels became orthodox around the middle of the 2nd century. The gospels that bear the name of these four apostles are traditionally said to have been written by them, but that has never been confirmed; additionally none of the original writings have been found for further study.[147] At this point, most scholars agree that none of the gospels – including the four mentioned here – were written while Jesus was living, and there is no evidence in the text that the original writers had ever been in his presence (James may be the exception and the Book of James, although not a gospel, could have been written as early as 40 CE).[148]

There has been renewed scholarship to focus on the strength of oral traditions and a push to end the divide between the "Historical Jesus" and the "Christ of Faith."[149] Even so, most biblical scholars date the earliest Gospel of Mark at some time after 70 CE and the last Gospel of John after 90 CE, which would be between 40 to 60 years after the alleged crucifixion. The Catholic Church traditionally portrays these authors as the apostles Mark, Luke, Matthew and John, even though there is no evidence for this. In fact, many bibles are labeled as the Gospel according to St. Mark or St. John, which is chronologically inconsistent with the Church's later practice of conferring sainthood.

The texts of Matthew and Luke appear to have derived in large part from Mark, or all three of them from an earlier, as of yet unknown, source referred to as Q (from the German word Quelle, meaning "source").[150] The Gospel of John disagrees with events described in Mark, Matthew, and Luke and was written in Greek near the end of the first century. Of Mark's 666 verses, approximately 600 appear in Matthew and half that number in Luke. The author of Luke admits that he is not an eyewitness to the events described.[151] Luke, not unlike Paul and many of the other New Testament authors, was probably a Romanized Jew (although the name Luke itself is of Greek or Italian origins).

Sometime in the middle of the first century, Paul, of Tarsus (modern-day Turkey), converted to Christianity from a sudden mystical experience on the road to Damascus, where he had planned to root out Christians for punishment (Acts 9:1-30). Paul's letters to the early Church make up half of the New Testament and are the primary source of early Church doctrine. His major contribution to Christian theology was his idea of a new covenant in which anyone who professed faith in Jesus Christ could participate.[152] This new covenant (hence "new testament") allowed anyone to partake in it, as opposed to the "old covenant" that was strictly between the Abrahamic descendants and God. His primary effort, as seen in his numerous letters to the gentile (non-Jewish) communities of his day, was to offer a version of Judaism to his Romanized contemporaries that they could accept and understand.

Nietzsche, despised by many modern Christians, went so far as to suggest Paul was responsible for constructing a new Christianity. He discussed what he viewed as Paul's frustrations at being unable and unwilling to comply with the Jewish law of the time and therefore conveniently used Christianity as a means of destroying that law. Nietzsche is more famous – and loathed – however, for his oft quoted statement "God is dead," which has hence lent itself to the ever-popular bathroom graffiti "God is Dead, sayeth Nietzsche," always followed by "Nietzsche is dead, sayeth God!"

It is unlikely the early Christian Jews like Peter, James, and John would have understood themselves as founding a new religion, but more likely saw themselves as reforming Judaism from within. They would have recognized many of the Jewish holidays, circumcised their sons, and kept kosher dietary restrictions.

In Paul, however, we see a de-emphasis on the law and emphasis on faith when he says in Romans 3:28, "For we hold that a man is justified by faith apart from works of law." Or Corinthians 10:25, "Eat whatever is sold in the meat market without raising any question on the ground of conscience." This is in stark contrast to what Jesus is professed to have said in Matthew 5:17: "Think not that I have come to abolish the law and the prophets; I have come not to abolish them but to fulfill them."

Paul's concept of salvation has been accused, unfairly by some, as being more in keeping with Greek and Horite myth than anything in the Old Testament. Other critics of the New Testament have trouble reconciling what they see as contradictory key doctrinal passages within its own texts. Take Paul, for example, who says in Romans 10:9, "If you confess with your lips that Jesus is Lord and believe in your heart that God raised him from the dead, you will be saved." Compare this, however, with what Jesus is alleged to have said in Matthews 7:21, "Not everyone who says to me, 'Lord, Lord,' shall enter the kingdom of heaven, but only the one who does the will of my Father who is in heaven." Also, James – thought by some to be the half-brother of Jesus or an original apostle – says in the Book of James 2:26, "For as the body apart from the spirit is dead, so faith apart from works is dead."

Extensive discussion and arguments within Christianity regarding God's message in the form Jesus – his life and crucifixion – continued for centuries after his death. As a case in point, Gnosticism – or the belief that the material world is created by an emanation of the highest God trapping the divine spark in the human body – became quite prevalent. According to the gnostic Gospel of Judas (dating to approximately 200 CE), God is a "luminous cloud of light" who created Adamas (Adam) in His own image before Adam acquired his human form, by which humanity eventually began to forget its divine origins.[153] According to biblical historian Elaine Pagels, the gospel describes that in death, all of humanity rejoins this divinity: "we step into the infinite world of God, into the divine light, and we go into that glorious light with God."[154]

In addition to Gnosticism, there developed an early dispute about whether Jesus was collectively the son of God, God, and

God's spirit together, or that Jesus, as begotten of God, was separate from God and therefore did not always exist but was created. The latter view was championed by Arius, a Christian leader in Alexandria. His ideas were eventually considered heretical by an official edict of the first council of Nicaea in 325 CE held at the request of the Roman emperor Constantine. Constantine did not necessarily care about the theological differences or debate, but rather wanted to resolve the dispute one way or the other. Ultimately the doctrine of the trinity prevailed and all other views were considered heretical thereafter, including the gospels of Judas and Barnabas.

The Gospel of Barnabas has been referenced as a lost gospel, but there is evidence pointing to a possible later forgery or creation. The alleged gospel does not have Jesus dying on the cross but shows Judas being placed in his stead. It denounces the divinity of Jesus but affirms him as prophet, and it proscribes circumcision. Some have pointed out specific references to 15th century origin (such as wine being contained in wooden caskets instead of the flasks and pottery that would be customary in 1st century Galilee).[155] This may make the authenticity problematic.

If indeed a 15th century work, the general consensus is that these copies of the Gospel of Barnabas (with the possible exception of a recently discovered Aramaic copy) were written to somehow curry favor with Muslims of their time (even though many of its exegeses are contrary to Islamic tenants). Verse 4, section 147 of the Quran makes it clear why: "They say 'we killed Christ Jesus the son of Mary, the Messenger of Allah'—but they killed him not, nor crucified him, but so it was made to appear to them, and those who differ therein are full of doubts, with no (certain) knowledge, but only conjecture to follow, for of a surety they killed him not—nay, Allah raised him up unto Himself; and Allah is Exalted in Power, Wise."[156] As such, most Muslims reject the crucifixion narrative, but not all agree. For instance, even biblical scholar Reza Aslan, himself a converted Muslim, paradoxically believes the historical Jesus was in fact crucified. Aslan, on the other hand, freely admits there are few facts about Jesus we can be certain of – other than he was an historical figure who was targeted for execution due to his radical beliefs.[157]

Aslan agrees the gospels are meant to de-emphasize Jesus' Judaism. He also understands what we consider modern orthodox Christianity was just one of a multitude of competing religious and political Christian ideologies which were banned by Roman seats of power at the council of Nicaea, who declared all other beliefs heretical.

Reza Aslan relates that he was influenced and moved by Dostoevsky's *The Brothers Karasmovnov*, particularly the grand inquisitor's passage. Ivan, the atheist, tells his brother Alyosha, the believer, about the story of Jesus coming back during the inquisition and being arrested and sentenced to death by burning. The night before his sentence he is visited by the grand inquisitor who tells him he is unwelcome and his return is undermining the mission of the church, whose function is to preach. Aslan understood this passage to mean we must not confuse manmade institutions with faith.[158]

What would Moses say if he visited Jerusalem and the world's synagogues? What would Jesus say if he visited the Vatican and the world's churches? What would Muhammad say if he visited Mecca and the world's mosques? What would they all say, with peace and blessings upon them, about the educational institutions that have become the bastions of power and authority for practicing and administering faith?

All of them brought a message unique to their time and community but all with a purpose of instilling a love and respect for and obedience to God. However, over time institutions have developed that appropriate and modify these messages for purposes beyond – sometimes even contrary to – the letter and spirit of their original messengers. Deconstruction and syntheses of their core message – belief and devotion to one God, and living a life in peace and harmony – is often lost in translation, interpretation, denomination, or simply the convoluted minutiae. As Christian mystic Meister Eckhart noted, "if you focus too narrowly on a single path to God, all you will ever find is the path."

There are numerous contradictions found in the writings of the Old Testament. There are numerous contradictions found in the New Testament. And there are even more contradictions between the two, even when citing to the same event. As proof, former youth pastor Daniel Henson in his self-proclaimed "Dossier of Reason" does a fair job of documenting them and has found no less than 56 historical and geographical errors in the Bible, 34 scientific inaccuracies, 40 unfulfilled prophecies, and hundreds of internal inconsistencies.[159]

Henson, in the preface to his dossier, poses the problem of predisposition and why it is critical to "approach your faith of choice with objectivity and skepticism and not confirmation bias." He ponders whether a Muslim born in Saudi Arabia, given an objective look at Christianity, could accept it as true, and wonders if it is self-evident why more Muslims do not accept it as true. And further, if you could be exposed to all religions at once, how could you come to the conclusion that the one you believe in is true and all others false?

Henson posits that there is no evidence or argument that can positively demonstrate the existence of a god. But proofs (as Father Copleston and Bertrand Russell agreed) are no more absolute in science than in the act of belief. They are, instead, points on a scale of probabilities. And there are arguments that raise the probability of an intelligent designer (just as there are those hypotheses that lower such probability).

When we analyze the Old and New Testament, we have a hint of hope, and some would say a glimmer of truth, but also a serious handicap. Some of their books were not made part of their official cannon until decades, even centuries, after their purported revelations. We have no assurance they are true representations of their original message. But is this because they are manmade forgeries, or pure myth – or is it because they are the product of surviving revelations with possible omissions, or accidental or intentional alterations or additions?

The best preserved and most recent professed revelation of the world's great monotheistic religions is found in the Quran. Whether it is the word of God is a matter of faith, but its authenticity has little doubt.

11

Islam

"You cannot open a book without learning something."
~ Confucius

The Quran, from cover to cover, is made up of 114 chapters and 6,346 verses, which is roughly the same size as the New Testament. It is recorded just as it was revealed to, and recited by, the Prophet Muhammad ﷺ beginning the last days of the month of Ramadan in 610 CE, until his death in 632 CE. The Quran makes a distinction between it and the previous scriptures of the Jews and Christians, which it recognizes specifically as the Torat and Engeel, and not more broadly what today would include the Talmud and all the letters of the New Testament. Similarly, to properly analyze Islam it is important to distinguish its core message (the Quran) from later explanation or commentaries on its text (known as tafsir) and the recollection of stories and sayings attributed to Muhammed and his companions (known as hadith). All of the stories, commentaries, even later legal rulings in all three monotheistic religions are important, but they are not of the same character and primacy as their original messages.

Muhammad, an Arab bedouin born in 571 CE and reputed by some to be illiterate, was orphaned at a very young age at the death of his mother and father. He was placed in the care of his grandfather Abd al-Muttalib (known for discovering the ancient lost well of Zam Zam still flowing in modern-day Mecca). Shortly after taking in Muhammad, Abd al-Muttalib also passed away, and the care and protection of the would-be Prophet passed to his uncle Imran (better known as Abu Talib). At the age of 25 Muhammed married a wealthy Meccan business woman named

Khadijah, approximately 15 years his elder. When he was forty years old, he received his first divine revelation, of which others followed. The messages he received embodied the core concepts and values of Islam (stressing, among other things, both peace and submission). Amongst the first converts were Khadijah, Ali, and Abu Bakr.

Muhammad's companions wrote down what he said onto a variety of materials such as papyrus, stones, palm leaves, wood, animal skins, etc. These revelations were also memorized by his early followers and there has been to this day unbroken successive generations of hafiz (individuals who memorize and recite the entire Quran word for word). The first religious leaders of the Muslim community made efforts to collect and centralize these various fragments of the Quran, but it wasn't until the third leader of Islam, Caliph Uthman, that the whole Quran was finally assembled, approved, and widely disseminated throughout the Muslim world.

After the Prophet passed away it was agreed through consensus that Muhammad's close friend Abu Bakr would be caliph followed by Omar, Uthman (of the Ummaya clan), then Ali, Muhammad's cousin and son-in-law. But out of growing dissatisfaction with his leadership, Uthman was assassinated by his rivals. As a result, there grew a rivalry between the Prophet's widow Aisha (supported by Uthman's cousin Muawiyah) and Ali. The former wanted Ali to avenge Uthman, who was executed at the hands of a small number of Ali's supporters. Those supporters initially identified themselves as Shia Ali (party of Ali) and later just Shia.[160] Ironically, Ali was assassinated by a hard-liner Shia who believed Ali himself was being too conciliatory to his rivals and soon thereafter Muawiyah claimed the caliphate, ushering in a new Muslim dynasty.

The Umayyad dynasty lasted until 750 CE. The rise of the Abbasid dynasty was gained with the assistance of Shia forces. In the centuries that followed Shia Islam gained influence, and groups adhering to esoteric interpretations of Shariah (Islamic law) began to flourish. The Fatimids, a branch of Shia Islam, gained such prominence and influence that for a time they controlled all of Egypt, established Al Azhar, the first Muslim University, and even rivaled the rulers of the Abbasid dynasty. At around the same time Nizam al-Mulk, the grand vizier of the Seljuq dynasty

(Oghuz Turkish dynasty), developed an education system called "*Nizamiyah*" that emphasized religious studies at the expense of independent inquiry. The purpose of these learning institutions, including one where Al Ghazali taught (only to later leave out of frustration), was to counter those growing non-Sunni influences.

Although most scholars accept the traditional account of Islam and how it came about, even those who question the narrative have trouble explaining an alternative. For example, revisionists such as Patricia Crone, professor of history at Princeton – who portrays Muhammad as "a preacher in the Old Testament tradition hailing the coming of a messiah" – admits that the Quran and the Islamic tradition "present a fundamental paradox." The Quran is:

> filled with stories and references to Abraham, Isaac, Joseph and Jesus, and yet the official history insists that Muhammad, an illiterate camel merchant, received the revelation in Mecca, a remote, sparsely populated part of Arabia, far from the centers of monotheistic thought, in an environment of idol-worshiping Arab Bedouins. Unless one accepts the idea of the angel Gabriel ... historians must somehow explain how all these monotheistic stories and ideas found their way into the Koran.

For Crone there are only two other possibilities: "Either there had to be substantial numbers of Jews and Christians in Mecca or the Koran had to have been composed somewhere else."[161]

Some have theorized that the Quran was derived from Christian Aramaic sources in the early 8th century in an effort to evangelize the Arabs and became mistranslated later. By way of illustration, Christoph Luxenburg writing under a pseudonym proposed that the word "*hur*," which means white raisin in Arabic, had been mistranslated by later Arabs into the Arabic word "*houri*," which means virgin.[162] This has been widely discounted and is contrary to the other references to the houri having wide eyes, voluptuousness, and chastity. And of course, it is unlikely that men can be married to white raisins. On the other hand, it is possible that later interpretations may have different meanings than originally intended.

Early copies of the Quran are written without vowels and diacritical dots that modern Arabic uses. Studies in early Islam show that not until the 8th and 9th century did Islamic scribes and commentators routinely add these grammatical marks in an attempt to clear up ambiguities of the text. Gerd Puin, of Saarland University in Germany, has shown that in the earliest copies of the Quran, it is virtually impossible to tell the difference between the word to fight or to kill. Only later Muslims fixed its meaning to kill rather than to fight.

During the restoration of the Great Mosque of Sana in Yemen in 1972, some of the earliest known Quran fragments were found in a "Quran graveyard" of old Islamic Quran manuscripts. One of the fragments, making up approximately a fourth of the Quran, contained Quranic text written over an earlier version of the Quran. Puin was allowed some of the first access to the fragments and remarked at a number of differences between the earlier and later version. Later his wife, Elisabeth Puin, and others have had an opportunity to examine and comment on the variations between the two. Mrs. Puin has noted handwritten corrections (which she terms the lower modifiers) in the earlier version made before the whole text was erased or washed off. The differences, even though negligible, do occasionally include the addition of whole words and phrases.

Puin and others have suggested that the variations, although slight, are due to its evolving over time. However, it is well accepted that before Caliph Uthman ordered verified copies of the Quran that at least two other non-Uthman standardized copies of the Quran were kept by companions of Muhammad, including ibn Mas'ud and Ubayy ibn Ka'b. Puin and others have noted the differences between the lower text and those of ibn Mas'ud, but others such as Behnam Sadeghi and Mohsen Goudarzi have noted the many similarities, suggesting they may have been derived from an earlier unauthenticated version. Also, the handwritten corrections strongly suggest they were made to make the unverified version conform to those of the Uthman version.[163]

Tarif Khalidi, Palestinian historian at the University of Beirut in Lebanon, holds that the traditional Muslim account of the Quran's development is still quite accurate: "I haven't yet seen anything to radically alter my view." He and colleague Alexander Jones, Quranic lecturer at Oxford, believe the Sana Quran could have been a version that people originally had access to but did not know was inaccurate. "It's not inconceivable that after the promulgation of the Uthmanic text, it took a long time to filter down," Khalidi asserted.[164] The carbon dating on the Sana copies for the earlier text is said to be between 578 and 669 CE, to within 95% accuracy.[165]

An even earlier partial fragment was recently discovered at the University of Birmingham in 2015. It appears to be two leaves from another 16 held at the National Library of France in Paris. The two leaves have been carbon-dated and translated for comparison to the texts of the modern Quran. The fragment has been carbon-dated to between 568 and 645 with a confidence of 97.2% accuracy. It contains part of Surahs 18, 19, and 20. It has been found to be (minus grammatical marks for stressing long or short vowels) virtually identical to the matching surahs of today's Qurans read throughout the world.[166]

David Thomas, professor of Christianity and Islam at the University of Birmingham, states:

> The tests carried out on the parchment of the Birmingham folios yield the strong probability that the animal from which it was taken was alive during the lifetime of the Prophet Muhammad or shortly afterwards. This means that the parts of the Qur'an that are written on this parchment can, with a degree of confidence, be dated to less than two decades after Muhammad's death. These portions must have been in a form that is very close to the form of the Qur'an read today, supporting the view that the text has undergone little or no alteration and that it can be dated to a point very close to the time it was believed to be revealed.[167]

Keeping in mind that the Prophet is said to have passed away June 8, 632 CE, and Uthman June 17, 656 CE, these findings are quite remarkable, pointing further to the primacy and authenticity of the current and original texts.

Although there is little evidence of the text of the Quran changing over time, some modern Islamic revisionists, both Muslim and non-Muslim alike, are finding rather more traction in highlighting the changing interpretation of the Quran over time. Research reveals that interpreting parts of the Quran "metaphorically rather than literally ... [was] widely practiced in mainstream Islam a thousand years ago" compared to today.[168]

As Andrew Rippin, late professor of Islamic studies at the University of Victoria in Canada, has emphasized, "When I teach the history of the interpretation it is eye-opening to students the amount of independent thought and diversity of interpretation that existed in the early centuries of Islam. It was only in more recent centuries that there was a need for limiting interpretation."[169]

Mohammed Arkoun, the late Algerian professor at the University of Paris, argued in his *Lectures du Coran* that "it is time [for Islam] to assume, along with all of the great cultural traditions, the modern risks of scientific knowledge," and believed "the problem of the divine authenticity of the Koran can serve to reactivate Islamic thought and engage it in the major debates of our age."[170] Arkoun, like the late professor Rippin, regretted "the fact that most Muslims are unaware that a different conception of the Quran exists within their own historical tradition."[171] This problem is peculiar considering the opening chapter and verses of the Quran describe the provisions of heaven as allegorical likenesses to those provisions we now enjoy, and then states:

> God does not disdain from presenting any kind of allegory or example even of a mosquito or what is lesser or greater than that. As for those who have believed, they know it is the truth from their Lord. As for those who have disbelieved, they say, "What does God want to teach us by this example?" He misleads many thereby and guides many thereby. And he misleads not except the defiantly disobedient. (Q 2:26)

Many Muslims very early on developed a mistrust of philosophy and too free an interpretation of Islam. They aimed to curb the increasing reliance on external sources for understanding the Quran during that period. Because the Quran and the traditions of the Prophet were seen as containing all that was necessary for issues of ethics, meanings and morals, discourses in philosophy were thought of as mostly unnecessary or potentially dangerous.

In the first two hundred years following the revelation of the Quran, there developed three distinct groups competing for the authoritative source of legal decisions. They came to be known as the *ahl al ray* (advocates of common sense), *al kalam* (speculative theologians) and *al hadith* (advocates of following the example of the prophets). The party of al hadith ultimately prevailed. As previously mentioned, hadith are sayings and accounts of the Prophet and his companions, said to have taken place during their lifetimes. However, like the New Testament, many of these sayings and accounts were collected and recorded long after the events they purported to describe and do not have the same strength or claim to authenticity reserved for the Quran.[172]

Out of the Kalam School arose the rationalist school of Islamic theology known as Mutazali and its followers, Mutazalis or Mutazalites (though they personally referred to themselves as al tawhid or people of monotheism and justice). Even though they used logic and Greek and Indian philosophy, they remained grounded in the basic tenets of Islam. A major bone of contention between them and their rivals, the Asharites, was their refusal to accept that the Quran was eternal; instead, they said it was created. They denied the attributes of God were distinct entities and stressed free will. Al Ashari was the founder of asharihay, amongst the foremost theological schools in Sunni Islam. He and his students insisted reason must be subordinate to revelation.

Mutazilites say God is under an obligation to fulfill promises to reward the righteous. But Asharites say no, God can if God wants to reward the wicked or punish the believers. Asharites de-emphasized free will which would limit the sovereign freedom of the Creator. In time, due to the growing diversity of early Islam as society changed, there also grew a fear of too free an interpretation of Quranic texts because of lack of Arabic, distortion in meaning of verses, falsification of hadith, and excessive ijtihad (making legal decisions by personal interpretation of the Quran and hadith). For these reasons there arose a demand for a framework or methodology for Islamic jurisprudence.

Mohamed al-Shafi was the first Islamic scholar to formally record his legal principles, known as *usul fiqh* (jurisprudence), such as consensus and analogical reasoning in his treaty called Al Risala. Ahmed Hanbal, al-Shafi's pupil, developed the traditionalist school of jurisprudence following only the Quran, Sunnah (example of the Prophet) and views of the Prophet's ﷺ companions. It is the smallest and strictest of the Sunni schools and that adopted by the Wahhabi school of thought including modern Saudi Arabia.

Imam Hanifa, of the ahl al ray party, also followed the Quran and Sunnah but emphasized hypothetical situations for rulings and putting things in their context. He was accused of too freely following his own opinion, but he defended his approach as a safeguard against strict analogies that would be contrary to the Quran's objectives. The Maliki School relied on rulings that were consistent with the Quran and Sunnah but emphasized those primarily in the public interest.

Abu Hamid Al Ghazali, born in 1058 CE in what is today modern Iran, was one of the most influential philosophers, jurists, and mystics of Sunni Islam. Al Ghazali has been affectionately named by numerous Muslim scholars, including Sufi master al Haddad, as "proof of Islam."Al Ghazali's book The Incoherence of the Philosophers sought to counter the influence of philosophy, particularly Greek thought and metaphysics that was becoming so influential in his day.

Juwanni, Al Ghazali's master, came up with rulings that laid out the divine lawgiver's intent. He looked at intention and the effective cause of each ruling to extract its higher intent. Al Ghazali, although from the Shafi School, also supported the opinions of Malik. Al Ghazali, building on his teacher's works, named five objectives of the law: preserving religion, life, reason, progeny, and property. That one of the five included reason counters accusations that Al Ghazali was primarily responsible for the decline of rational Islam. There are a number of more important factors that accelerated this outcome, the foremost of which included the institutionalization of religious studies (primarily islamic jurisprudence) for the first time by the efforts of the "good vizier" Nizam al Mulk. Graduating from the Nizamiyah schools then was akin to getting a Harvard law degree today with promises of a lucrative career. Whereas as before science and Islamic law were commonly intertwined, after Nizam al Mulk they were generally more separated.

As a result, some recent scholars, such as Tariq Ramadan, have advocated for reform in Islamic jurisprudence that emphasize a more holistic approach to Islamic scholarship and jurisprudence that recognizes a book of the world on equal or primary footing with the later book of revelation.[173]

For Ramadan the universe itself must be considered as an autonomous and complimentary source of legal elaboration. "The revealed Book," he says, "neither stifles nor directs the mind, it liberates it at the heart of the Universe: the world speaks by itself, autonomously, and it is human intelligence's task to understand its language, its vocabulary, its semantics, its rules, its grammar, and its order."[174]

He believes Muslims have come to overuse the term "Islamic," for what is Islamic in a field are the ethics, norms and goals that orient and limit the use of the knowledge acquired.[175] He does not believe in Islamizing modernity, for neither Western civilization or Islamic civilization is a monolith. Both were mutually cross-fertilized, he says, and new generations of Muslims will only serve to reinforce this trend.[176] The goal: "We must reconcile ourselves with the world to be better reconciled with ourselves."[177]

PART III

RECONCILING SCIENCE AND RELIGION

-A-

LITERAL AND FIGURATIVE INTERPRETATIONS OF RELIGIOUS TEXTS

12

Contradictions and Confirmations

"We are now approaching lunar sunrise, and for all the people back on Earth, the crew of Apollo 8 has a message that we would like to send to you.
In the beginning God created the heaven and the earth.
And the earth was without form, and void; and darkness was upon the face of the deep. And the Spirit of God moved upon the face of the waters.
And God said, Let there be light: and there was light.
And God saw the light, that it was good: and God divided the light from the darkness."[178]

~ Transmission by Astronaut William Anders on December 24, 1968, while first orbiting the moon (quoting Genesis 1-4).

There are numerous scientific inaccuracies leveled at various passages in the Old Testament, New Testament and Quran. While some may have natural or even scientific explanations, others just don't seem to hold up to scrutiny or are clearly in error. This can be seen when we find references to the sun going around the earth. For instance, when the stars in their course fought against Sisera (affecting the outcome of a battle).[179] This is not in keeping with our Copernican understanding of our solar system.

In Isaiah 30:27, there is a reference to the light of the moon being as bright as the light of the sun and the light of the sun sevenfold, but because this is a future event, we cannot say with certainty this would be impossible. For if the light is referring to the moon's reflection of light then increased candescence of the sun would also bring a proportional luminosity of the moon.

In other instances, some men of ages past were apparently both excessively large and lived excessively long. For example, Methuselah apparently was as old as 969 years.[180] A race of men called the Amorites were giants as tall as cedars.[181] However, although unlikely, by current anatomical and biological understanding this is not entirely impossible.

Some recent studies have suggested there is an upper limit to the aging process at around 105 years old. This is the age when the human death rate starts to plateau, while generally the rate increases exponentially until age 80.[182] Demographic data from nearly 4000 Italians above 105 showed that with each passing year they were no more likely to die than they had been before reaching that age. Professor Jim Vaupel, who was a scientist on aging at the Max Planck Institute for Demographic Research, said, "evidence points towards no looming limit … if there is a limit it is above 120, perhaps much above – and perhaps there is not a limit at all."[183] Even if there is currently some biological upper limit at around 120 years, it does not mean that this was always so.

The story of giants may be more problematic but, again, not entirely impossible. There have been numerous 19th century reports (hundreds) of giant skeletons unearthed from ancient burial mounds across America ranging from seven to ten feet tall.[184]

Other criticisms include a flood of global proportions that covered every mountain top.[185] And taking every beast, cattle, insect, and bird of every sort onto the ark.[186] The geological record does not show total global deluge since the appearance of mammals in the late Triassic period about 200 million years ago. And with a zoological record in the millions for every epoch man has been on earth, gathering them all on an ark would be a virtually impossible feat to accomplish. There simply would not be enough room or time to preserve every animal on earth on a single boat of any reasonably conceivable size. That the flood was only regional would account for it flooding local surrounding mountaintops, but there is no evidence of flooding above the Himalayas with peaks over 7000 meters high.

The archeological record does support significant flooding in the Mesopotamia area around 5,000 years ago, as well as a monumental emptying of the rising waters of the Mediterranean into the low-lying areas around the modern-day Black Sea some 7500 years ago. These events, though rare, when they do happen are significant. Keep in mind the modern Mediterranean was once a desert spotted with scattered areas of salty ocean. At some point in the distant past the Atlantic Ocean rose to where it eventually spilled back into the former sea. Such an event would have been quite impressive. The subsequent deluge that enveloped the Black Sea area was so massive it is estimated to have created a waterfall 200 times the volume of the Niagara Falls whose roar could have been heard more than 100 miles away.[187]

Some have disputed the story of Moses leading captive Jews out of Egypt, parting the Red Sea, and the Israelites wandering in the desert for 40 years when they could have gone from Egypt to Israel in months. However, modern archeology firmly places pockets of Jewish encampments in ancient Egypt in and around the lower Nile delta, coinciding with the biblical Exodus. And just because one can get to an area in weeks or months, especially by modern estimations, does not mean that such displaced people on the move necessarily did so or had the means, inclination and opportunity to do so at the time. Equally there have been plausible theories postulated how a shallower, marshy, reed-covered body of water prior to its draining by the construction of the Suez Canal could have, under the right meteorological conditions, allowed temporary crossing.

In the Gospel of Mark, we read at Jesus' crucifixion that darkness covered all the land for three hours and a great earthquake shook temples and opened graves, causing many dead bodies to arise and walk through the city.[188] No record independent of the gospels themselves preserves such extraordinary events. Solar eclipses do not last for that duration and any earthquake and mass resurrection would likely have garnered some note from the Roman prefects of the time. Additionally, the crucifixion is described as occurring at the time of Passover in Matthew 26:2. Passover occurs during a full moon while eclipses can only occur during a new moon when it is passing between the earth and the sun. It is confidently calculated that a partial lunar eclipse happened on April 3, 33 CE, but such an event would only have temporarily darkened the moon and not the entire land.

Genesis, because it provides a unique and fascinating account of our cosmological origins, allows interesting potential revelatory insights or clear fallacies. One with a modern understanding of the cosmological formation and biological evolution is struck with Genesis' many conformations of these concepts and, at once, its contradictions.

For example, Genesis 1:1-9 describes what sounds somewhat like a flat-earth explanation for the universe's early beginnings. God is described as hovering over the waters which were formless and empty and dark, and then produces light on the first day. On the second day God separated the waters with water above and below, and the resulting area between them the sky. On the third day God let the water under the sky be gathered in one place called seas, and the dry ground that appeared in its midst, called land.

In Genesis 1:11 God then produces vegetation and seed-bearing plants and trees, also on the third day. On the fourth day, God creates the sun, the moon, and the stars. On the fifth day God lets the waters teem with living creatures and lets birds fly above the earth across the vault of the sky.[189] On the sixth day God let the land produce creatures such as livestock, crawling creatures and wild animals and then man, who was to have dominion over the other creatures.[190]

This is a quite remarkable account consistent with life on earth forming progressively on land (in the form of plants), then oceans, and then animals on land eventually to the point where mankind is said to share some of God's attributes, including that of dominion, due to their advanced intellect, understanding and consciousness.

It is true that not all creatures in the ocean first formed in the ocean, such as sea alligators, whales and dolphins, etc. But since it is understood that land bearing creatures likely later adapted to life in the sea, this in itself is not problematic. The problem arises in the order when compared to our modern understanding of the fossil record.

Some of the first sea sponges formed around 640 million years ago. Although fossil specimens of flying fish have been found to have lived over 240 million years ago, the first insects, including those of the terrestrial variety, lived about 412 million years ago at about the same time terrestrial plants appeared. Not until 153 million years ago do we get evidence of the earliest flying bird, *Archaeopteryx lithographica*, a bird of crow-sized proportions, the remains of which were found in Jurassic sediments in Germany. Thus, terrestrial insects existed long before the first flying birds, or even flying fish. But both flying fish and especially birds developed long after the ocean was first teeming with life.

The first flowering plants did not occur until around 200 million years ago and the first grasses about 66 million years ago. In this sense the account, while generally accurate, is still problematic. Even if you accept the reference to flying birds may be a mistranslation for flying insects, formation of the sun and stars after the earth and before plants can in no way be reconciled by modern astronomy and archeology, and the need for photosynthesis for plants from the light of the sun. For you see in Genesis 1:14 that the lights in the heavens included the lesser light of night (stars and the moon) and the greater light of day (the sun) were all made on the fourth day (after grass and trees and fruits were made).

On the other hand, up until very recently the scientific community had commonly accepted that life began in the oceans first, not on land as Genesis states. But now some scientists think "molecules essential for the origin of life would be dispersed too quickly into a vast ocean" and its salinity would inhibit the conditions for life to begin. Instead, stromalites have been discovered in the western Australian desert, giving evidence there were living organisms there 3.5 billion years ago. It was once thought they were formed in shallow, salty seawater. But recent research shows they were formed in conditions similar to the hot springs of Yellowstone Park. This discovery pushes the origin of microbial life on Earth back by 580 million years and strengthens the groundbreaking hypothesis proposed by UC Santa Cruz astrobiologists David Deamer and Bruce Damer. According to their theory, life did not originate in the sea but rather on land.[191]

The most glaring inaccuracy in the Genesis account, of course, is the entire formation of the heavens and earth, and all creatures within it, in 6 days. Scientists and astronomers estimate the universe is at least 13.7 billion years old. Days could have easily been a reference to units of times or periods and thus proportional and not figurative, and yet the order of the creation is not as it is now understood. Because Genesis was written long after the events it describes, and most likely long after the alleged revelations were first given, it is easy to see how alterations and mistranslation could have been introduced to the story.

The Quran, which has been accused of both borrowing from Judaism and Christianity and altering it, provides some interesting insights to the Genesis story. In the Quran, it states, like Genesis, that God created the heavens and the earth and all that is between them in 6 days. It uses the word "youm" or day. In some instances it relates that the measure of a day is equal to 50,000 years (70:4), and in another that a day in the sight of your Lord is like a thousand of your reckoning (22:47), tending to show that the word youm can be understood to refer to a long period of time or an era or eon.

Because the Quran proclaims to confirm and add to the earlier prophetic messages, it may be postulated that it can explain the era or eon understanding of "day" in Genesis rather than the literal day as commonly understood. But where the Quran may save the Genesis literal 6-day account, it appears to adopt at least in part the apparent erroneous primordial dark water universe if not its flat-earth insinuations. But some explanations may be in order.

In Surah Hud 11:7, the Quran states, "And He it is who created the heavens and the earth in six days (eons) – and his position of authority *was* upon the water." The general translation is that the "throne" (position of authority) is referred to in the past tense. This has been explained that once the heavens and earth were fully formed, the throne then became over the heavens and earth where it still remains.

In Ayat Al Kursi – one of the most well-known and regarded by some as the most powerful verse of the Quran – it states in part: "He knoweth that which is in front of them and that which is behind them, while they encompass nothing of His knowledge except what He wills. His throne *includeth* the heavens and the earth, and He is never weary of preserving them."[192] Here, his throne is spoken of in the present tense and now includes, or extends, over the heavens and earth as we currently know it, insinuating that which God rules has changed in character while the rule continues. It may be that the water in Surah Hud is a reference to earth, or it may be referring to the early period of the formation of the universe. The Rashad Khalifa translation of Surah Hud 11:7, as discussed above, is: "He is the One who created the heavens and the earth in six days – and his (earthly) domain was completely covered in water."

Researchers from the Australian National University in their 2017 study revealed that around 4.4 billion years ago the earth was once almost entirely covered with water without mountains or tectonic plates. Their findings also suggest it remained this way for a long time, perhaps as long as 1.5 billion years.[193]

Some looking at Surah Hud and Genesis (as well as other creation stories) have speculated that the water designated in their accounts is referring to some primordial substance from which all things emerged, a kind of fluid or liquid that has potential but not quite formed.[194] Perhaps the water we drink is symbolic of this primordial water.[195] When the Quran speaks of God's *Arsh* (which means throne or power) in this context it is described as being above the water or, in other words, in a realm that has dominion or control or power over this primordial fluid or undifferentiated substance.

In a study published September 26, 2014, in *Science*, researchers found that up to 50% of the water on earth today was formed before the swirling dust and gas that gave rise to our planets and solar system. Its lead author, Ilsedore Cleeves, an astronomer from the University of Michigan remarked, "It's pretty amazing that a significant fraction of water on Earth predates the sun and the solar system." According to the study, some of the H2O in our tap water and oceans were created more than 4.5 billion years ago.[196]

This helps the Genesis version, but at the same time the water Cleeves and her colleagues are referring to – although more abundant than originally thought – is still just a fraction of the total of hydrogen atoms thought to be common throughout the universe then and now. Also, they would have at one point been ice crystals (at least when the earth began to form) floating and swirling throughout the primordial nebula. These findings may give the Quranic and biblical references renewed consideration, but fall short of definitive proof. When the scriptural verses are clear, the veracity of their claims are somewhat easier to verify. But, often as is the case, the differences come down to interpretation and even translation.

A prime example is Surah 79:27-30 of the Quran. It states in part, "Are you more difficult to create than the firmament (*samma*) ... He made dark its night and set forth its morn, and the earth, after that He spread it wide (*dahaha*)." In the Rashad Khalifa version we have: "Are you more difficult to create than the heaven (samma) ... He made its night dark and brightened its morn. He made the earth egg shaped (dahaha)."[197] By using the meaning of dahaha – spread it wide – some have supposed this is a flat-earth perspective. But by using the term egg-shaped, it is clearly a round earth analogy.

The use of the word dahaha is not common but has context in classical Arabic. Its root word *daha* or *duhya* has several meanings. It can mean causing it to move or to roll; it also can mean round or spherical (*dahaa*). For instance, in one hadith Osama, a companion of the Prophet, is described as having a round and big (dahaa) tummy. *Dahiya* still is used today as the noun for egg. In its verb form, daha can mean to expand, or less commonly to shape like an egg. In the form *dihya* it means powerful or exalted.

Sama means sky. *Samawatin* means skies. Sometimes the translation is firmament or heaven(s) or universe. Occasionally it means clouds or rain (such as a cloudy sky). It generally depends on the context. In the above verse, it appears to refer to the immediate sky overhead, which is part of the greater universe (or by most interpretations the lowest layer of the seven universes) in the layered heavens.

By these various translations we get the sense of the earth being round or rolled, being expanded into the shape of an egg in connection to the creation of the earth and the sky, the heavens and the firmament. Most translations, however, still prefer using the narrower spreading out definition of the verb. In fact, there is a persistent anecdotal rumor that even so lofty a figure as the former Grand Mufti of Saudi Arabia, Abd al-Aziz bin Baz, prior to his appointment had proclaimed rather emphatically that the earth is flat, only to be critically and repeatedly satirized for his belief.

According to British historical author Robert Lacey, "the sheikh was unrepentant. If Muslims chose to believe the world was round, that was their business, he said, and he would not quarrel with them religiously. But he was inclined to trust what he felt beneath his feet rather than the statements of scientists he did not know." According to Lacey, it was not until bin Baz spoke to Prince Sultan bin Salman Al Saud – former air force pilot and payload specialist aboard the STS-51-G space shuttle mission in 1985 – who assured bin Baz the earth was indeed round, that the *sheikh* retracted his position.[198] Sometimes it's not the translation that is questioned; rather it's the phenomenon it is describing that is not clear.

In Surah Fussilat, the formation of the heavens and earth is described as follows: "Do you really disbelieve in him who created the earth in two eons … and after creating the earth he set mountains rising above it and blessed it, and in four eons (in all) equitably apportioned upon it the sustenance for all who would seek it (two periods to form and two periods to make habitable)" (Q 41:9-10).

In Surah 41:11-12 it states, "Moreover (Thumma) He applied His design to the heaven which was as yet smoke and said to it and to the earth, 'Come the both of you [into being], willingly or unwillingly.' They said, 'We have come willingly.' Then He decreed that there be seven heavens in two eons and ordained each heaven its unique law. And we ordained the heaven of the world [the lowest layer] with lamps and protected it."

By this account a third of the universe's creation consisted of the forming of the early universe (the heavens and their first stars), one third for forming the earth, and one third for the forming of life on earth. Or one third to form the first stars and two thirds to form later Population I stars and the planets, including earth.

Consistent with the Big Bang theory of the universe the Quran states, "And the sky (samma) we constructed with our power and will continue to expand it" (Q 51:47).

It is interesting to consider that, by both the scriptural and scientifically documented accounts, the materials comprising the universe were once homogenous. "Do the disbelievers not see that the heavens and the earth were joined together, then I split them apart?" (Q 21:30).

By these scriptural accounts (if we assume the universe is around 15 billion years old) it took close to 5 billion years to form the universe with Population II stars (which are older and do not have the mineral and elements necessary for carbon-based life), then a little less than 10 billion years to form the sun and earth. If you include the accretion and dissemination of raw material in and around our solar system – which may have taken close to 5 billion years – and then include the appearance of land masses, mountains, and tectonic drift and formation of life that has occurred over the past 4.5 billion years, then the 6 days/eons revelations (1/3, 2/3 proportion in the Quran) deserve some consideration. By such calculations, one may find the scriptural correlations to recent scientific cosmological understandings either surprisingly close or at least plausible.

Astronomers are puzzled why with the known density of matter in the universe it continues to expand when it should eventually contract under its own gravitational pull. As discussed earlier, to explain this expansion they predict almost 70% of the mass in the visible universe is made up of dark energy. NASA scientists have determined that, assuming the density of the universe is very close to the critical density (the density needed for gravity to stop expansion of the universe), then the geometry of the universe is roughly flat, like a piece of paper.[199]

The Quran describes the coming of a day when God will "fold up the heaven like the folding up the pages of a book [or closing of a scroll], as we begin the creation so too shall we bring it forth again. It is a promise that is binding upon us. Truly we shall fulfill it."[200] In Surah Nuh it is asked, "See you not how Allah has created the seven heavens one above another, and made the moon a light in their midst, and made the sun as a [glorious] lamp?"[201] In Surah as Saffat, 37:06, it states, "We have indeed decked the lower heaven with beauty [in] the stars." Therefore, we assume there are other heavens or uppermost layers beyond that in which we have the observable stars in the known universe.

It is not universally agreed what the seven heavens is referring to (such as in the verses above and throughout the Quran). But because they are described in layers – with the heaven of the world as having lamps, and the lowermost heaven with stars – most agree that the first heaven is the universe with its vast expanse of stars, including the sun burning like a lamp and the moon reflecting its light at night. Therefore, it may suggest that in some as yet unknown realm at the outer boundary of our universe there lies many more heavens or realms presumably without visible stars. If the universe were being pulled and stretched along with energy and mass (of unknown densities) at its outer boundaries, it might provide an alternative explanation (other than repulsion by dark energy) for its accelerated expansion. Keep in mind only 5% of normal matter makes up the stuff we detect in our universe. By modern estimates, ten times the current density in the universe would be required to counter the observed expansion of the visible universe.[202]

Hadith may provide additional insight. Even though most hadith were not recorded until much later than the events they attest to, they may serve to illuminate a particular subject or cast doubt on it. Some hadiths were thought to have been borrowed or influenced by contacts with Jews and Christians as the Islamic empire extended. Therefore, they have to be viewed with appropriate caution, but sometimes with equal fascination.

For example, in one such hadith about the seven heavens, Abu Hurayrah narrated:

> The Prophet asked, "Do you know what is between you and it?" On their replying that Allah and His Messenger knew best, he said, "Between you and it are five hundred years."
>
> He then asked, "Do you know what is above that?" On their replying that Allah and His Messenger knew best, he said, "Two heavens with a distance of five hundred years between them." He went on speaking like that till he counted seven heavens, the distance between each pair being like between Heaven and Earth.

> He then asked, "Do you know what is above that?" On their replying that Allah and His Messenger knew best, he said, "Above that is the Throne, and the distance between it and the [seventh] heaven is the same as that between each pair of heavens … and nothing is hidden from Allah of your deeds.[203]

In another narrated by Al-Abbas ibn Abdul Muttalib, perhaps referring to the same discussion, the Prophet said, "… The heaven which is above it is at a similar distance (going on till he counted seven heavens). Above the seventh heaven there is a sea, the distance between whose surface and bottom is like that between one heaven and the next. …"[204]

This last hadith is reminiscent of the Genesis story. Therefore, it is either borrowing from the story or elaborating in some sense on an earlier revelatory truth. This includes suggesting that the vault of the heavens contains concentric rings of space, each with its own laws of physics where the outermost layer is enveloped in a vast expanse of water (or some other viscous substance) between it and the vault. In the Quran this region is referred to as the *Kursi* (or the chair to the throne) and God's throne the Arsh. By another hadith narration this region is as vast as the Sahara Desert relative to a ring (which represents the diameter of the Arsh and seven heavens) thrown in its sands.[205]

In some descriptions the other heavens increase in size, and perhaps density, as one travels through them. In others they are roughly uniform. If indeed the universe is flat, then so too may these additional heavens. If the universe is round, then the heavens could be in concentric layers, not unlike the layers of an onion, with our universe at the center and us at some prime if not central location. For what wonders lie within them one can only imagine. On the other hand, of course, if you discount these accounts altogether, they are just fanciful tales of the past.

There are a plethora of inconsistencies and fallacies leveled at the Quran, and in particular hadith, just as they have been leveled against the Old and New Testament. Many of them arise out of a misunderstanding or are squarely addressed while others remain uncertain or unanswered. In addition to those already referenced, there are multiple other verses that appear to describe various processes that we are only recently able to understand, verify, and appreciate regarding weather cycles, botany, reproduction, embryology, weather patterns, geology, and astronomy to name a few. Most famously French physician Maurice Bucaille was amongst the first to document some of these in his novel book, *The Bible, The Quran and Science* (La Bible, Le Coran et la Science) first published in 1976.[206] However, one of the biggest current points of contention leveled at Christianity and Judaism, even Islam to a lesser extent, is the theory of evolution. One that is incorrectly believed to have started solely with the works and research of Charles Darwin.

13
Islam and Evolution

"Low in the earth
I lived in realms of ore and stone;
And then I smiled in many-tinted flowers;
Then roving with the wild and wandering hours,
O'er earth and air and ocean's zone,
In a new birth,
I dived and flew,
And crept and ran,
And all the secret of my essence drew
Within a form that brought them all to view– And lo, a Man! . . . "[207]
~ Rumi

The Quran reveals early in its opening chapters that God told his heavenly hosts, including the angels, "'I am placing a representative on Earth.' They said, 'Will you place therein one who will spread evil therein and shed blood, while we sing your praises, glorify You, and uphold your absolute authority?' He said, 'I know what you do not know.' Thereafter he taught Adam the names for which the angels had no knowledge."[208] He then told Adam and Eve, "Dwell you and your wife in the Garden/ Paradise (*Janata*) and eat thereof generously as you please but do not approach this tree, or you will be of the wrongdoers."

Prior to their eviction from the garden the Quran states, "Therein there is neither hunger nor (the sense of) nakedness, neither suffering from thirst therein nor exposure to the heat of the sun" (Surah 20:118-119). This reference to the heat of the sun may give a clue to the whereabouts of this splendid garden paradise.

But Satan (amongst the first of the creatures known as *jinn*) caused them to slip. As we know Adam disobeyed and ate from the tree that Satan suggested would grant him and his wife eternal life, and upon doing so they "became conscious of their nakedness, and they began to cover themselves with leaves from the Garden" (Q 20:121). Whereby God said, "Go down [all of you], some of you to others [as] enemy; and for you in the earth [is] a dwelling place and a provision for a period" (Q 2:35-36).

There is a debate whether Adam and Eve were first residing in a place not of this earth and then removed to earth, or whether the garden they were first in was always here on earth. When we take the view that man was created instantly and not evolving slowly over a time, it is easy to see how these verses interpret Adam and Eve's early stay in the garden/paradise being in an otherworldly place. Particularly when coupled with other Quranic references describing the paradise of the afterlife as having rivers, gardens, and fruits and drinks without depletion or end. However, when you find in the Quran verses that appear to support evolutionary development of mankind on earth, then the argument that the early garden was in fact an earthly garden gains more support. For why would man be evolved on earth slowly to then be removed and then placed back on earth as a sort of punishment for disobedience?

The Arabic word for go down (*ih'bitu*) in verse 2:36 is also used elsewhere in denoting an earthly relocation. Verse 2:61, for example, relates how the Israelites, who are wandering through the desert with Moses, begin lamenting over the succulent cucumbers, lentils, garlic, and onions they once enjoyed back in Egypt. In response, God asks whether they would rather return to their original situation, and if so then to "Go down (ih'bitu) to Egypt where you can find what you asked for."[209]

That Islam and the Quran support evolutionary biology is not a new or novel idea. In fact, it well predates the theory offered by Charles Darwin, and may have even given him the impetus for some of his ideas. The word "scientist" was not part of the common vernacular before the 1800s. Only with the rise of scientific and intellectual endeavors did there develop a perceived conflict between science and religion. Out of this arose a conflict thesis which maintained there is an intrinsic intellectual conflict between religion and science, which naturally leads to hostility.

One staunch proponent of this perceived conflict was 19th century English scientist John William Draper. Draper, a contemporary of Darwin, openly described natural selection as "Mohammedan [*sic*] theory of evolution":

> Theological authorities were therefore constrained to look with disfavor on any attempt to carry back the origin of the earth to an epoch indefinitely remote, and on the Mohammedan [sic] theory of the evolution of man from lower forms, or his gradual development to his present condition in the long lapse of time.[210]

Draper's assertion of the Islamic origins of evolution is for good reason, since there is a clear historical connection.

Al Jahiz, a 9th century Mutazili Muslim from Iraq, lived from 776 to 869 CE. He wrote *The Book of Animals*, which helped advance the zoological sciences. He believed that the transformation of species and mutation was possible. He appears to be amongst the first Muslim scientists to recognize the effect of environmental factors on animal development, and observed the transformation of animal species under different factors. He also described the struggle of existence for survival, its aims and mechanisms. He wrote about the mechanisms for evolution as the struggle for existence, the transformation of species into each other, and environmental factors.[211]

Ibn Miskawayh, an 11th century Iranian and Zoroastrian convert to Islam, was one of the first to clearly describe the idea of evolution. Muhammad Hamidullah describes the evolutionary ideas found in Ibn Miskawayh's *al-Fawz al-Asghar* (The Small Achievements) as follows:

> [These books] state that God first created matter and invested it with energy for development. Matter, therefore, adopted the form of vapour which assumed the shape of water in due time. The next stage of development was mineral life. Different kinds of stones developed in course of time. Their highest form being mirjan (coral). It is a stone which has in it branches like those of a tree. After mineral life evolves vegetation. The evolution of vegetation culminates with a tree which bears the qualities

of an animal. This is the date-palm. It has male and female genders. It does not wither if all its branches are chopped but it dies when the head is cut off. The date-palm is therefore considered the highest among the trees and resembles the lowest among animals. Then is born the lowest of animals. It evolves into an ape. This is not the statement of Darwin. This is what Ibn Maskawayh states and this is precisely what is written in the Epistles of Ikhwan al-Safa. The Muslim thinkers state that ape then evolved into a lower kind of a barbarian man. He then became a superior human being. Man becomes a saint, a prophet. He evolves into a higher stage and becomes an angel. The one higher to angels is indeed none but God. Everything begins from Him and everything returns to Him.[212]

Arabic manuscripts of *al-Fawz al-Asghar* were available in European universities by the 19th century. It is believed to have been studied by Charles Darwin, himself a student of Arabic. If so, it is easy to imagine it, and other such writings, had some impact or influence on his evolutionary theories.[213]

Al Tusi, a prominent 13th century Ismaili Muslim Iranian scholar, philosopher and scientist, also believed in evolution. His theory of evolution did not begin, though, with organic biology. It was more comprehensive. He saw the universe as consisting of uniform elements that became differentiated through time, eventually developing into minerals, plants and animals. It included a theory of survival of the fittest:

The organisms that can gain the new features faster are more variable. As a result, they gain advantages over other creatures. … The bodies are changing as a result of the internal and external interactions.

It also included the theory of natural selection and adaptation.

Look at the world of animals and birds. They have all that is necessary for defense, protection and daily life, including strengths, courage and appropriate tools [organs] ... Some of these organs are real weapons … For example, horns-spear,

> teeth and claws-knife and needle, feet and hoofs-cudgel. The thorns and needles of some animals are similar to arrows. [...] Animals that have no other means of defense (as the gazelle and fox) protect themselves with the help of flight and cunning. … Some of them, for example, bees, ants and some bird species, have united in communities in order to protect themselves and help each other.[214]

Ibn Khaldun, a North African Arab of the 14th century, was a historian and widely considered to be the founding father of modern sociology and economics. He is also regarded as one of the greatest philosophers of the Middle Ages. In his all-encompassing book *The Muqqadima* he describes evolution. Ibn Khaldun asserted that humans developed from "the world of the monkeys," in a process by which "species become more numerous." In Chapter 1 of *The Muqaddimah* he states:

> … this world with all the created things in it has a certain order and solid construction. It shows nexuses between causes and things caused, combinations of some parts of creation with others, and transformations of some existent things into others, in a pattern that is both remarkable and endless. …
>
> One should then look at the world of creation. It started out from the minerals and progressed, in an ingenious, gradual manner, to plants and animals. The last stage of minerals is connected with the first stage of plants, such as herbs and seedless plants. The last stage of plants, such as palms and vines, is connected with the first stage of animals, such as snails and shellfish which have only the power of touch. The word "connection" with regard to these created things means that the last stage of each group is fully prepared to become the first stage of the next group.
>
> The animal world then widens, its species become numerous, and, in a gradual process of creation, it finally leads to man, who is able to think and reflect. The higher stage of man is reached from the world of monkeys, in which both sagacity

> and perception are found, but which has not reached the stage of actual reflection and thinking. At this point we come to the first stage of man ... This is as far as our [physical] observation extends.[215]

Even though the Quran is not generally thought of as a science book, it does have numerous verses that can be interpreted to support the theory of evolution. The following are just a sample of some of the more relevant passages:

Q 21:30-30: "Do not the Unbelievers see that the heavens and the earth were joined together [as one unit of creation], before we clove them asunder? We made from water or liquid [*ma*] every living thing. Will they not then believe?"

Q 24:45: "And Allah has created every animal or moving creature [*dabbatin*] from water [ma]: of them there are some that creep on their bellies; some that walk on two legs; and some that walk on four. Allah creates what He wills for verily Allah has power over all things."

Q 71:13-17: "Why should you not revere God seeing that it is He that has created you in diverse stages [*atwaran*]? Do you not see how Allah has created the seven heavens one above another, And made the moon therein a light and the sun a Lamp? And Allah has caused you to grow gradually [*anbatakum*] from the earth, as a plant grows [*nabatan*]."

In the Quran the material used to form man is specified by different names, such as soil (turab) in the initial stage. Then clay (salsalin) in an intermediary stage. Then with a reduction in water content and left to age, sticky black mud (hama-in). Soil content, like the composition of humans and animals, includes carbon, hydrogen, nitrogen, calcium, phosphorus, sodium and a host of other elements. There may be other life forms, as the Quran suggests, but we know these elements are necessary to develop and sustain the carbon-based life forms that we are more familiar with, including ourselves.

Q 3:59: "Adam ... He created from the dust [*turab*, fine dry particles of earth or soil] ..."

Q 15:26-27: "We created the human being from clay [*salsalin*] from black mud [*hama-in*] fashioned or altered into shape [*masnunin*]. And the jinn, We created before of intensely hot smokeless fire."

As this last verse suggests, other intelligent beings have been created out of non earthly substances, such as the jinns from smokeless fire[216] (plasma readily fits this latter description).[217]

By these verses one can clearly see support for a theory that prior to Darwin's theory had come to be coined "Mohammedan [*sic*] evolution." They may go even further in describing in basic terms what has come today to be termed abiogenesis (the theory of how living organisms evolved from inorganic substances). These verses notwithstanding, not all Muslims agree. In fact, it may be fair to surmise that many if not most Muslims do not. Some modern Muslim creationist authors like Harun Yahya[218] have written extensively on the subject in rejection of the theory, particularly "random mutation" and "natural selection." Yahya points to the problem of a lack of intermediary transitional forms. Darwin, he says, "was hoping that this problem would be overcome by new fossil findings. Paleontology, on the contrary, invalidated Darwin's theory more and more each day."[219] He even pokes fun at Darwin's suggestion that whales evolved from bears that tried to hunt in the sea. But apparently Darwin posthumously gets the next if not the last laugh. The fossil record now shows both hippos and whales shared a four-footed, semi-aquatic mammal that thrived over 40 million years ago as a common ancestor. There used to be an enormous gap between the fossils of early cetaceans and early hippos. However, in 2004 Jean-Renaud Boisserie and his colleagues in France announced they finally filled in the gap with fossils of water-loving animals that evolved into two groups, including early cetaceans and the anthracotheres that died out about 2.5 million years ago.[220] *Pakicetus*, a now-extinct four-legged genus of amphibious cetacean (which looks rather more like a bear than a whale) of the Eocene era, is now considered by virtually every paleontologist as the most basal whale. Although carnivorous, their skulls, particularly in the ear region, very closely resemble modern whales.

Yahya is rather more effective not in denying evolution in species but in invoking design:

> By believing that pure chance can produce perfect designs, evolutionists cross the bounds of reason and science. The famous zoologist Pierre Grasse, the former president of the French Academy of Sciences, makes his point about the logic of "chance", which is the backbone of Darwinism: "The opportune appearance of mutations permitting animals and plants to meet their needs seems hard to believe. Yet the Darwinian theory is even more demanding: a single plant, a single animal would require thousands and thousands of lucky, appropriate events. Thus, miracles would become the rule: events with an infinitesimal probability could not fail to occur. There is no law against daydreaming, but science must not indulge in it."[221]

It should be noted that there is a distinction between Muslims who disagree with the theory of evolution generally, such as Yahya, and those who disagree only with man and modern humans having evolved from lower primates. Most Muslims accept evolution generally while many still reject the latter.

Even a modern Islamic scholar, no less revered than Nuh Ha Mim Keller himself, found an opportunity to weigh in on the topic. Keller, a Christian convert to Islam and translator of a number of Islamic books, including *The Reliance of the Traveler* (hadith reference source), was authorized as a sheikh in the Shadhili order in 1996. On June 27, 1995, Suleman Ali, a biologist who was himself convinced by the evidence that supported evolution, asked whether Sheikh Keller agreed. In response, Keller summarized as follows after a rather lengthy explanation:

> Allah alone is Master of Existence. He alone causes all that is to be and not to be. Causes are without effect in themselves, but rather both cause and effect are created by Him. The causes and the effects of all processes, including those through which plant and animal species are individuated, are His work alone. To ascribe efficacy to anything but His action, whether believing that causes (a) bring about effects in and of themselves; or (b) bring about effects in and of themselves through a capacity Allah has placed in them, is to ascribe associates to Allah (*shirk*). Such beliefs seem to be entailed in the literal understanding

> of "natural selection" and "random mutation," and other evolutionary concepts, unless we understand these processes as figurative causes, while realizing that Allah alone is the agent. This is apart from the consideration of whether they are true or not.
>
> As for the claim that man has evolved from a non-human species, this is unbelief (*kufr*) no matter if we ascribe the process to Allah or to "nature," because it negates the truth of Adam's special creation that Allah has revealed in the Qur'an.[222]

If you accept that the principles of evolution are based on completely random circumstances that arise in nature then you, as Yahya charges, "foster the materialist philosophy which denies God."[223]

Researcher and lecturer David Solomon Jalajel, after carefully documenting both support and criticism for the theory of evolution amongst Muslims, concludes that "resistance is primarily due to an assumed association of evolution with 'Godlessness' and to a poor understanding of evolutionary principles, and is not so much due to strictly theological or scriptural considerations."[224]

Jalajel posits that biologists with and without faith can support a statement of the basic principles of evolutionary theory (that the "present diversity of living species came about as a result of gradual changes in the gene pools … whereby genetic variety was introduced to these populations by mutation and by other means and then acted upon by various factors such as natural selection"). They can do so because they are describing what they see in the observable world. But a biologist with faith, Jalajel says:

> …will do so with the certainty of faith that he is, to the best of his ability, describing God's creative process as he sees it taking place in the world around him. An atheist, on the other hand, will be convinced within himself that the processes he sees have no metaphysical dimension to them, no Intelligent Creator behind them.
>
> These two positions are ideological, metaphysical ones; neither of which is supported nor denied by the theory of evolution.

They are matters that the theory of evolution – and indeed science in general – is utterly unfit and unequipped to address.[225]

Some modern biologists have come to question whether it is even appropriate to look for "all-encompassing laws to describe the properties of biological systems" when they have arisen haphazardly. Evelyn Fox Keller, a physicist, biologist and philosopher, concludes as follows:

> By its very nature, life is both contingent and particular, each organism the product of eons of tinkering, of building on what had accumulated over the course of a particular evolutionary trajectory. Of course, the laws of physics and chemistry are crucial. But, beyond such laws, biological generalizations (with the possible exception of natural selection) may need to be provisional because of evolution, and because of the historical contingencies on which both the emergence of life and its elaboration depended.[226]

Natural selection requires genetic variation brought about by genetic mutation. Thus, not unexpectedly, its detractors ask: If nature is randomly selecting beneficial mutations in the gene, what is causing the genes to mutate in a more advantageous way? Why should genes mutate in beneficial ways and not in dangerous or defective ways? But nature itself answers. There are countless examples of various congenital defects due to chromosomal or genetic disorders, such as congenital heart disease, down syndrome, cleft lip, spina bifida, just to name a few. And of course, some are so detrimental that they prevent full gestation of the organism, which effectively ends that potential hereditary branch of the species (including its deleterious mutation).

Other detractors point to the lack of evidence for abiogenesis. The fossil record is hard to piece together from millions of years ago. It is even harder to piece together evidence from billions of years ago. This notwithstanding, the classic 1952 Miller-Urey experiment showed most amino acids (necessary for forming proteins used in all living organisms) could be synthesized from inorganic compounds. But since that time, no one has actually replicated either the conditions or the jump from inorganic to organic life. Some see this as a fatal flaw, but again they fail to see the slow incremental crawl of accumulative change and increasing complexity that involves molecular self-replication, eventually leading to the emergence of the cell membrane. Until recently there was no explanation for how carbon – the backbone of organic chemistry – could develop into phosphorus (another key ingredient for life as we know it). However, researchers at the Scripps Research Institute in California have now "identified a molecule capable of performing phosphorylation in water, making it a solid candidate for what has until now been a missing link in the chain from lifeless soup to evolving cells."[227]

A better question made by the proponents of intelligent design is, How do you account for complex specified information in nature? or How do you account for the presence of code in DNA? Perry Marshall, author of *Evolution 2.0*, makes a distinction between inorganic structures such as the sun and rocks and living organisms complete with DNA.

> Nature can create fascinating patterns – snowflakes, sand dunes, crystals, stalagmites and stalactites. Tornados and turbulence and cloud formations. But non-living things cannot create language. They *cannot* create codes. Rocks cannot think and they cannot talk. And they cannot create information. It is believed by some that life on planet earth arose accidentally from the "primordial soup," the early ocean which produced enzymes and eventually RNA, DNA, and primitive cells. But there is still a problem with this theory: It fails to answer the question, "Where did the information come from?"[228]

He is referring explicitly to complex information. There is a difference between complex information and simple information, and information that is both complex and specified.

For example, American mathematician William Dembski has formulated a universal probability bound to set a threshold beyond which the culmination of an event cannot be afforded to chance alone. This he applies to what he coins complex, specified information. Hence when such an object or event is identified it infers design as an explanation (irrespective of the identity of the designer). As a design detection theorem, it may arguably be used (assuming the probabilistic statistics are accurate) to infer design in cosmological and biological observations. Despite being rife with critics it does offer some formula whereby empirical evidence might discount natural selection and Darwinian Evolution as the only explanation for complexity in living organisms.

Although all substance contains information, natural selection through random mutation is hard pressed to account for this coded information. The emergence of bio information during natural processes of evolutionary development in species and organisms cannot be explained by current physics and biology. Increasingly modern researchers and theorists are coming up with possible answers. "Because natural selection selects beneficial mutations and beneficial mutations are those which satisfy the criteria of bio-intelligence, they are not random. Bio-intelligence is the origin of human intelligence, i.e., 'The nature of intelligence is nature's intelligence.'"[229] This reasoning sounds circular but there is little way around its conclusion. How you characterize the origins of this natural intelligence, though, is open to interpretation.

There still remains a disconnect between those who believe in a higher omnipotent force sustaining nature on the one hand and those who believe nature itself is the only force molding its own constituencies without the hand of God. They are both adopting too narrow and at the same time too superior a position. The materialists see organisms and consciousness as emergent qualities that have no preconceived essence, thus denying God. The theists rail at the notion of organisms constantly changing, such that man, like animals, is just another momentary train stop on a slow, random route, thus somehow taking away from his sanctity.

Science is increasingly confirming this slow route with its incremental changes, but neither its possible destination nor the ultimate means of locomotion (except pure circumstance). Even if you accept that man is the current end product of countless mutations and adaptations, it does not take away in any way from his sanctity or special place. For Man is without question at the apex of evolutionary development, the most advanced and complex carbon-based (and phosphorus-based) life form the world has ever seen. Whether it is done at the hand of God slowly, or all at once, is a matter of faith and interpretation, but by a critical look at the actual texts of the Quran, one can certainly make a strongly supportive theistic argument for a process akin to modern evolutionary biology. If other religious texts also do, or once did as well, then one of modern atheism's strongest tools for cutting down belief becomes quickly ineffective.

Modern Darwinian evolutionary biology sees a means without an end as an agent for biological change, but it does not see how the means is connected to the whole or why. How and why are questions it cannot answer, and some even say should not be asked because its meandering course cannot be predicted. But if that were the case, then all of science's efforts to make reasonable predictions, with its many diverse branches, would equally prove fruitless. For who knows what tomorrow brings. Instead there are fairly predictable laws at work of which we see their effects. There are countless others that have not yet been revealed but one day will. There are yet others, that surely, we will never come to know. What is so compelling about evolution, though, is it does not just work for biological systems; it is the prevalent and predictable outcome of all matter in motion.

Mulla Sadra, an early 17th century Shia philosopher, abandoned Aristotle and Plato's essentialism in favor of an existentialist philosophy. Whereas preceding philosophers had accepted change only in quantity, quality, position and place, he saw change as the all-pervasive norm driving and transforming all reality including substance itself. Sadra's "doctrine of substantial motion is founded on the idea that all elements in nature, including celestial bodies, experience significant change and transformation due to the inherent flow and permeation of existence. This process, known as 'self-flow' (*fayd*) and the penetration of being (*sarayan al-wujud*), bestows upon each distinct individual entity its portion of existence."[230]

For Sadra, existence is a continuous unfolding of a unified whole with a constantly evolving manifold. We only imagine that objects have an essence when capturing a snapshot between changing modes of existence. Sadra "saw that the world – that is, every spatio-temporal event from the highest heaven downwards – is thus temporally originated, although as a whole the world is also eternal in the sense that it has no beginning or end, since time is not something existing independently within which the world in turn exists."[231] In other words, Sadra – amongst the most prominent Islamic philosophers of the last 400 years, otherwise mostly obscure to the rest of the non-Persian world – foresaw the relativity of time and space, comprehensive evolution, and was a pioneer of pure existentialism. Sadra, even though he was not a scientist per se, was nevertheless quite effective at reconciling theological doctrine and discourse such as the Quran and its commentaries with the intellectual sciences of his day.

-B-

THE UNIVERSE AS AN EMANATION OF GOD'S WILL

14

From Socrates to Sadra: the search for objective truth

"God and nature create nothing that does not fulfill a purpose."

- Aristotle

Our view of reality and understanding of the world we live in is in a constant state of flux. Most would agree the world itself is in a constant state of flux and change. But Mankind has ever expressed a desire to find the constant and unchanging (stability), behind or underlying the ever-changing (dynamic).

Various societies in their early development – in building an understanding of the world in which they lived – believed in unseen forces at play, some of them permanent that influenced the known and observed world in which we live. It was common in premodern cultures to see the world in both a logical and mythical way (what the ancient Greeks called the mythos and logos). Even though they existed in their own separate sphere they were considered complementary and essential, each serving their own important function. Myth is described by historian Karen Armstrong as a useful form of psychology that has fallen into ill repute:

> … in the past, myth was not self-indulgent fantasy; rather, like logos, it helped people to live effectively in our confusing world, though in a different way. Myths may have told stories about the gods, but they were really focused on the more elusive, puzzling, and tragic aspects of the human predicament that lay outside the remit of logos.[232]

For Armstrong the symbols, rituals, and myths are very important, providing something profound for which we seemed to have lost.

Similarly, Spanish-American author and philosopher George Santayana understood religion's higher purpose of strengthening man's soul by contemplating a more harmonious, perfect, and beautiful world. For Santayana God is the embodiment of our highest human aspirations. For him the value of religion does not depend on it being the literal word of God but rather an ideal guide for how to live our lives. Although an atheist Catholic, he believed in the superior value of ritual over belief (even remarking that in this regard Protestantism, with its emphasis on belief alone, had set religion back a good ten centuries). For Santayana religion is not science but rather inspirational poetry.[233]

Modern science is built on the belief that permanence is not to be searched for in unseen gods, or God, or heavenly hosts, but in natural laws that can be hypothesized and verified through experimentation and proof. The best-preserved documentation of this process is seen in the writings of the early Greek philosophers. At that time there was a battle being waged between what is good and just and what is true, between relative truth and absolute truth. On the one hand were the Sophists and rhetoricians, and on the other were Socrates and Plato and the dialecticians.

The Sophists were rhetoricians who used persuasive arguments to achieve their just and good goals. But Socrates, even though he learned from the Sophists, began to despise them for their lack of concern for the truth. The Sophists were first and foremost teachers, and many of the best students were aspiring lawyers. They taught their students so they could make equally persuasive and good arguments on either side of a particular issue, whether in aid of a plaintiff, prosecutor or a defendant.

Socrates and his followers were concerned with the pursuit of truth and knowledge and the establishment of virtue and good character. The place Socrates sought knowledge and truth was not in the world around him as the early philosophers before him had stressed, but within man himself. It was Socrates who helped define the concept of the soul which he described as one's capacity for intelligence and character or one's conscious personality. Socrates' favorite method for culling out the truth, in what we say and mean, was dialogue. A discourse on a particular subject in which the questioner and subject mutually must arrive at objective truths that neither one can disagree with.

It is interesting to find this Socratic method is now used extensively in Law Schools across the country as the primary means of teaching law in the classroom, and also is used in the courtroom in that part of the trial known as direct and cross examination of witnesses for establishing the facts or truth of the case. The ironic result being that in a modern trial the methods of both the Sophists' persuasive argument and Socratic dialogue are combined for culling out the truth and the facts (direct and cross examination), and then to persuade your audience (the jury) to accept your interpretation of these facts (opening and closing argument).

Socrates' greatest contribution to the modern world was his insistence on objective or absolute truth over subjective or relative truth. He believed that vice was ignorance and knowledge was virtue. Even though Socrates believed that people committed evil acts, he did not believe anyone did an evil act because he knew it to be evil. Wrongdoing to Socrates was an inaccurate expectation that certain kinds of things will produce pleasure or happiness. Because Socrates believed that the fundamental nature of man was unchanging, he believed that expected behavior and morals were unchanging also.

Socrates had his best student in Plato, and it is from Plato that we come to know so much of Socrates. But it is not Plato who has contributed so much to western thought and science as his student Aristotle. Aristotle wrote an important philosophical paper called metaphysics or "after physics" in which he was concerned about a type of knowledge which he considered wisdom or first philosophy. Wisdom involves trying to understand the first causes or principles which go beyond the subject matter of the various sciences, and looks not at the knowledge of any particular object or activity but knowledge of reality itself. It is knowledge at the highest level of abstraction and is concerned about what is universal instead of what is particular. He was concerned about the process by which specific substances come into being. Why?

Aristotle had a meticulous habit of classifying and categorizing the various substances and beings he found in nature. His desire to know how these various distinct substances, plants, animals, etc. were brought into being, later came to be the foundation for modern science and the scientific method. It is from this point of departure that greater effort was put into finding permanent universal laws that affect natural phenomena than permanent eternal unseen forces at play such as primitive and intuitive notions like gods or God.

What Socrates and Aristotle were proposing that was so revolutionary, was looking for true reality and objective truth both within ourselves and outside ourselves. It is through our knowing, rationalization, logic, and deeper understanding that we can come to know the true nature of the world. It is not in any imaginary, emotive, mythical explanations. They protested those who would play on people's emotions (such as the Sophists) to arrive at agreed upon truths instead of careful observations, abstractions, and logic. They put more trust in observations than feelings (particularly Aristotle, for even Socrates believed that true happiness was a goal in and of itself).

The truth was more important than the good or immediately expedient (even though Socrates in some simplistic way thought to know the truth would be to do the good). So powerful were these ideas of objective truth and scientific method that they helped in part to advance the golden age of Muslim learning with Arab interpretations and contributions to the Greek philosophical texts – and in turn allowed Europe to begin to emerge from its dark ages and spawned the Renaissance.

But it seems this scientific revolution came at a cost. In the words of Robert Pirsig, "man … had built empires of scientific capability to manipulate the phenomena of nature into enormous manifestations of his own dreams of power and wealth – but for this he had exchanged an empire of understanding of equal magnitude: an understanding of what it is to be a part of the world, and not an enemy of it."[234] Our pursuit of objective truth, although refining technological mastery, has also led to a diminished appreciation of our intrinsic connection to the world as a whole and our proper place in it.

Mulla Sadra, like Pirsig, was an existentialist process philosopher. Sadra is a link to the past and signpost to the future for new attempts at harmonizing religion (particularly Islam), science, and philosophy. He questioned the motives and methods of Islamic scholars of his time, and expounded upon this dissatisfaction frequently. He believed many of the scholars of his day and of days past were men who merely aspired to power and influence. Who were often more concerned with their legal exegesis than they were of genuine understanding of God or revelatory knowledge or, more importantly, the transformative power of all knowledge.

In a sense, Sadra believed like Socrates that knowledge of the good was the path to true happiness. But unlike most modern and post modern western philosophers who have followed, Sadra was not hesitant to supply the identity and the source of the good. For Sadra (like most Muslims) there was no question but of all good, all existence, having at its source the first being or wellspring of all being in God. But Man's purpose is not simply to profess allegiance to God and that God is good and thus in turn do good. It is for Sadra both simpler and more meaningful than this, for man – like all emanations from the reality that at its source is being – are either weaker or stronger manifestations of being, and all are in a continual process of perfection whose goal is to return to God from whence we all, and everything, has emanated.

Sadra saw substance as a manifestation of being and being as actualization. In this way reality is never completely stabilized in any particular *existant* (the thing that exists) but sets the existant into motion, into substance, toward ever higher modes of perfection. So each thing is currently only a degree of an ongoing actualization or process. In this framework time is not a mode for the unfolding of existence but is the result of the progression and intensity of substantial motion. Essential motion is an infinite potential mode of immaterial and absolute being. Sadra's substantial motion and

Pirsig's metaphysics of quality are not unlike Henri Bergson's *élan vital* or "vital impulse" which drives all organisms toward constantly more complicated and higher modes or organization.

Often it is asked, If Absolute Being is infinite and good or blissful, how could we have a world with limitations such as pain and suffering and death and evil? Typically, the Hindu answer would be that Absolute Being is not bound by its infinite consciousness and infinite bliss but has infinite diverse manifestations, sometimes even contrary, various forms of being. For Buhddists it would be due to attachment and ignorance. Both Taoism and Confucianism accept it is part of the human condition, and recommend how to navigate these challenges in harmony with the natural and moral order of the universe. More broadly, religion and philosophy answer that evil is a product of our own choice and free will. Because we are involved in a process of growth, our most profound evolution does not come from stillness, peace, or happiness but from pain, fear, setback, and difficulty.

Pain and suffering, even death, are part of a process. In fact, the process is all there is. For Sadra it is the means by which the soul is afforded, an opportunity to balance and temper its desires, to gain in identity from an undifferentiated spark and endeavor for excellence. In the words of English poet John Keats, "a World of Pains and troubles" is vitally necessary "to school an Intelligence and make it a soul ... A Place where the heart must feel and suffer in a thousand diverse ways!"[235]

Even if we can't all agree that nature and the universe are created, we can agree they have the characteristics of time and space, and substance, and constant change and progression. Nature by any estimation is permanent activity. It is also the substance of all things and the cause of their movement. Nature is thus the link between what is eternal and what is originated, and nature is originated both eternally and temporally. Because nature is ever-changing does not mean that recurring patterns do not emerge or exist.

We inquire of nature but we do not inquire beyond a limit of being's nature. Nature provides familiar patterns that give reality coherence, meaning, and stability, but nature and nature's existants are also constantly reconstituting and asserting themselves into new combinations and patterns that are vibrant and dynamic. This does not mean that objective truth does not exist, it only means that it always has to be searched for with a new light (without turning off the old one).

In nature essence is the sum of all experience which results from material interaction. Therefore, essence and existence in nature are inseparably intertwined. Things are animated and put into motion by non-tangible forces (energy, consciousness, etc.). The experience of these things interacting with other things defines their essence. Our perceptions, concepts and value judgments are part of the experience which adds to the sum total. In nature essence grows, as does material interaction.

The metaphysics of being is readily suited for explaining a universal intuitive knowledge of God (the nonphysical, nonobjective wellspring of being) in all of nature from mankind on down to the simplest inorganic elements. It offers a metaphysical framework for overlapping and complementary inquiries and advancement of our understanding in the fields of theology, science and philosophy. It readily explains the relationship between mind, body, and spirit. It shows consciousness is part of infinite fields of potential, waiting to be picked up by all receptors having a local transformative conscious experience. It is in such a framework that essence and existence co-exist, that everything flows from and is thus connected to the wellspring of being, yet that original source transcends all of nature.

In such a framework time is just a byproduct of substance in motion. For that which creates substance and uses it to affect a divine will, time and substance are not constraints. Nor is the arrow of time at microscopic levels. Physics tells us at this level, consciousness is involved in ferreting out classical reality. It is here where all choosers (or subsets of the chooser) have already freely decided outside of space and time, and the result of that choice is manifested simultaneously in space and time. Organic matter, inorganic matter, particles, molecules, plants, animals, us – we are all choosing in our own sphere of influence, seamlessly integrated by our parts to the whole, by the causes to the effects, contributing to the free and yet inevitable outcomes. It is by this metaphysical operation that fate and free will can harmoniously co-exist. Even though we are a subset of God (as are our choices), we are not co-equal with God.

The difference between the pantheistic view and the transcendent view appears to be a thin one, but there is an important distinction. The creation which is originated is synonymous with all individuals and subsets of that creation. However, God who creates but is not created is outside of this nature. The choosing consciousness may be part of a non-local unitive consciousness, but not everything is God or an aspect of God. It is not something that is conducive to scientific proofs. Instead, we sometimes are forced to rely on our intuition.

As Sadra suggests, similarly to Descartes, existence is an intuition that all intelligence possesses, which logically includes a necessary being, an absolute being. It is not arrived at by demonstrations of logical proofs, but rather such proofs reinforce faith in the one source of all being.

15

Reality: the greatest show in the universe outside of heaven?

> *"Miracles are a retelling in small letters of the very same story which is written across the whole world in letters too large for some of us to see."*
>
> ~ C.S. Lewis

Physicist John Wheeler believed the universe is made up of particles, fields and information. He coined the phrase "it from bit" to popularize the idea that the universe emanates from the information inherent in itself (in much the same way a computer processes concise bits of information). But if the nature of reality is information, it implies consciousness to comprehend and interpret it. According to Wheeler, we live in a "participatory universe," which emerges from the interplay of consciousness and physical reality.[236]

Information theorists like Wheeler and Claude Shannon believe the universe is about information processing, and matter is an emergent or necessary instrument for that process. Some have even suggested that our universe is merely an enormous simulation, perhaps even being projected like a 3D hologram from a 2D source. If so, it begs the question who or what is projecting the image. It would also provide early clues of a physical mechanism for an intelligent mind (God) converting will to reality, but it would also strengthen the argument for reductionism, or the belief that everything can be reduced to physics or processing of information at a particle or subatomic quantum level, including consciousness. It would show consciousness is really just a physical process, and traditional mind-body distinctions are illusory.

But even with advances in the understanding of the physical, chemical, and informational processes in the brain, those processes that may be taking place at the quantum level are, as of yet, still not fully understood. In fact, quantum mechanics in general still remains a bit of a mystery and has not been fully integrated with classical physics. But whether the universe is primarily energy, matter, information (or something else), is it something that exists independent of any other realm, heavenly or otherwise? If God is transcendent and exists outside the universe, how could we ever interact with God? If God is omnipresent, he is everywhere and thus cannot be transcendent.

Most ardent scientists do not believe in miracles or the supernatural. Only that there are things we can explain and things that we have yet to explain, and those things that we observe and cannot explain are mistakenly miscategorized as miracles or supernatural. On the other hand, virtually all those who profess a belief in God are convinced that there is an aspect of reality that is not physical or natural, but rather supernatural or spiritual without defining precisely what this spirit is or consists of. While a small minority believe God does not intervene in or interact with the creation (popularized by the deism movement of the 17th and 18th century), most still believe God is a supreme being and creator who exists independent of the universe but interacts with such creation, including humanity, as a supernatural deity.

But is it possible for a scientist to be a believer? One of today's leading scientists, Dr. Francis Collins – a former atheist and convert to Christianity, and head of the Human Genome Project – says yes and gives evidence in support in his popular book *The Language of God*. Others like George Cunningham say no and refute Collins' evidence. Collins believes that God is unlimited in space and time and takes a personal interest in human affairs, even on occasion miraculously.

Collins admits he was heavily influenced by the legendary Oxford scholar C.S. Lewis' book *Mere Christianity*. Lewis and Collins postulate that right and wrong are universal among all members of the human species. Interestingly, because Lewis sees God as being outside the universe, He could not show Himself to us in the universe any more than "the architect of a house could actually be a wall or staircase or fireplace in that house." Referring to moral law, Lewis conjectures:

> If there was a controlling power outside the universe, it could not show itself to us as one of the facts inside the universe ... The only way in which we could expect it to show itself would be inside ourselves as an influence or a command trying to get us to behave in a certain way. And that is just what we do find inside ourselves. Surely this ought to arouse our suspicions?[237]

Of this moral law Collins finds it ironic that Dawkins, who argues the gene's "relentless drive for survival ... explains the existence of all living things," also believes "we humans are at last far enough advanced to be able to rebel against our genetic imperatives."[238] Collins subscribes to evolution by God's will rather than the godless evolution ascribed to by Dawkins. Like Lewis, Collins supposes God, the architect of the universe, must somehow stand outside his creation.

> The major and inescapable flaw of Dawkins's claim that science demands atheism is that it goes beyond the evidence. If God is outside nature, then science can neither prove nor disprove His existence. Atheism itself must therefore be considered a form of blind faith, in that it adopts a belief system that cannot be defended on the basis of pure reason.[239]

Collins, like others, turns to Stephen Gould for support. "Science simply cannot by its legitimate methods adjudicate the issue of God's superintendence of nature. ... Science can work only with naturalistic explanations; it can neither confirm nor deny other types of actors (like God) in other spheres (the moral realm, for example)."[240]

Collins, instead of denying evolution to support his belief in God, points squarely at our common ancestry with chimps and apes. He does so by directing our attention to the presence of pseudogenes, genes that have almost all the properties of functional DNA but have one or more glitches that make their instruction unintelligible. One example is the human gene caspase 12, which is found in the identical relative location in the chimp. The gene works fine in chimps and all other mammals, but not humans. So, assuming "humans arose as the consequence of a supernatural act of special creation, why would God have gone to the trouble of inserting such a nonfunctional gene in this precise location?"[241]

Collins shows not only what makes us common with our evolutionary ancestors but what makes us different by pointing to the gene FOXP2. For three generations a single family in England had severe difficulty in speaking and processing words according to simple grammatical rules, and was unable to move various muscles to articulate sounds. Genetic detective work discovered "a single letter of the DNA code misspelled in the FOXP2 gene on chromosome 7." It was then discovered that the gene had remained stable in almost all mammals except humans, "where two significant changes have occurred in the coding region of the gene, apparently as recently as a hundred thousand years ago. The hypothesis suggested by these data is that these recent changes in FOXP2 may have in some way contributed to the development of language in human beings."[242]

Foreseeing that such discoveries could bolster the argument man has evolved without God, as an explanation Collins comments on what it means to be human:

> In my view, DNA sequence alone, even if accompanied by a vast trove of data on biological function, will never explain certain human attributes, such as the knowledge of the Moral Law and the universal search for God. Freeing God from the burden of special acts of creation does not remove Him as the source of the things that make humanity special, and of the universe itself. It merely shows us something of how He operates.[243]

Collins, after laying out the evidence for evolution, makes his case for theistic evolution re-branded as BioLogos. The basic components of the theory are: the universe came about roughly 14 billion years ago precisely tuned for life despite massive improbabilities; once life arose the process of evolution and natural selection permitted biological diversity over long periods of time with humans as part of this process, sharing a common ancestor with the great apes; humans are unique in ways that defy evolutionary explanation but point to a spiritual nature that includes the knowledge of right and wrong and a search for God that characterizes all human cultures.

One peculiar component of the theory is, "Once evolution got underway, no special supernatural intervention was required."[244] Satisfied with the basic components, Collins proposes renaming the theory "Bios through Logos" (BioLogos). This uses the Greek word for "life" and "word," or "life through word." Or, in this case the word of God. To punctuate the point, he quotes John 1:1: "In the beginning was the Word, and the Word was with God, and the Word was God." In other words, "'BioLogos' expresses the belief that God is the source of all life and that life expresses the will of God."[245]

In the Old Testament the "word" of God usually refers to scripture revealed by God, but it also implies something more. For example, in Isaiah 40:8 it states, "The grass withers and the flowers fall, but the word of God endures forever." Or Psalm 33:6: "By the word of the lord were the heavens established, and all the host of them by the spirit of his mouth."

Similarly in the Quran, God's word, will and action are synonymous. For God to affect his will, "All he needs to do to carry out any task is say to it 'be' and it is" (Surah Yasin 36:82). But the "word" cited by Collins is also referring to Jesus as the incarnation of God, as we see later in John 1:14: "The word became flesh and made his dwelling among us. We have seen his glory, the glory of the one and only Son."

Collins provides some evidence for God, such as "the fact that the universe had a beginning, that it obeys orderly laws that can be expressed precisely with mathematics," and a remarkable set of coincidences that allows the existence of life. Although he admits they "do not tell us much about what kind of God must be behind it all, but they do point toward an intelligent mind that could lie behind such precise and elegant principles."[246] Collins also admits, "Most of the world's great faiths share many truths … and each person needs to seek out his own particular path to the truth."[247] For him it was the acceptance of Jesus as the human incarnation of God, a personal and approachable God, rather than an obscure or theoretical deistic god.

This truth, however, seems to contradict the notion espoused by Lewis that, "If there was a controlling power outside the universe, it could not show itself to us as one of the facts inside the universe."[248] For Collins the explanation for the godly incarnation of Jesus and his resurrection, not unlike Moses parting the Red Sea, are miracles. These are events that are uncommon and do not happen every day, but if you admit like Collins that "there might exist something or someone outside of nature, then there is no logical reason why that force could not on rare occasions stage an invasion. On the other hand, in order for the world to avoid descending into chaos, miracles must be very uncommon."[249]

Lewis adds, "God does not shake miracles into Nature at random as if from a pepper-caster. They come on great occasions; they are found at the great ganglions of history... If your own life does not happen to be near one of those great ganglions, how should you expect to see one?"[250]

Lewis' choice of the word ganglion is instructive. Ganglions are a cluster of input nerve fibers that provide relay points, such as between the peripheral and central nervous system. Neural networks self-organize in nature. Instead of describing the universe as a simulation made up of information being projected somehow outside of the universe, it is possible to conceptualize it as a self-contained, mind-like neural network. Instead of nerve fibers, "the neural network can be made of symbolic geometric code" as the basis of an "information-only reality."[251]

According to code theorists such as Klee Irwin, the "information of this symbolic system would live in the emergent pan-consciousness that evolves from the evolution of this physical code. So the code exists or lives within the evolutionary emergent consciousness, which is self-actualized and emerges from the code."[252] Similarly, according to Christopher Langan's Cognitive-Theory Model of the Universe, "reality is a language that is talking to itself about itself."[253]

Langan, the modern genius of Malcolm Gladwell's popular book *Outliers*, theorizes that reality possesses a sort of self-awareness in some respects, like a mind. His theory states that mind and reality, subjective and objective, abstract and concrete are linked together. The mind of reality is, according to Langan, by mathematical and scientific definition, God. He proposes that our minds in connection "to the Mind of God ... is like the connection of parts to a whole, is what we sometimes call the soul or spirit, and it is the most crucial and essential part of being human."[254]

In Langan's theory, reality is both a kind of mind (of God) and language that contains multiple levels of consciousness. For Langan the soul is the connection of our consciousness embedded in the global consciousness of the universe as a whole. Conscious agents such as ourselves are "'sublanguages' possessing their own cognitive syntaxes. Now, global consciousness is based on a complete cognitive syntax in which our own incomplete syntax can be embedded, and this makes human consciousness transparent to it; in contrast, our ability to access the global level is restricted due to our syntactic limitations."[255]

Langan appears to share some affinity with Christianity when he admits souls may:

> attain a state of grace and partake of Systemic timelessness ('life eternal'). If, on the other hand, they do not – if they give themselves over to habitual selfishness at the expense of others and the future of their species – then they are teleologically devalued and must repair their connections with the System in order to remain a viable part of it. And if they do even worse, intentionally scarring the teleological ledger with a massive net loss of global utility, then unless they pursue redemption with such sincerity that their intense desire for forgiveness literally purges their souls, they face spiritual interdiction for the sake of teleological integrity.

Although his theory or worldview has elements of utility built into the system, notions of repentance or redemption more familiar with the Christian conception of salvation are present as well. Nonetheless it is otherwise quite comprehensive in its scope, and Langan himself admits that "Much of what we have been taught by organized religions is based on the illogical literalization of metaphorical aspects of their respective doctrines."[256]

In such a sense BioLogos, as life and reality emerging from the command or word of God as expressed in the Old Testament, finds some allies or at least similarities in modern theoretical models of nature and reality. But to hold that God came to earth in the form of Jesus the man to atone for all of mankind's sins does not necessarily logically follow. The Bible itself at times contradicts the doctrine, most notably John 10:30-38. In this passage Jesus says, "I and the father are one," which is so blasphemous it nearly invokes stoning by his audience. In response to their indignation he says, "Isn't it written in your law [referring to Psalm 82:6: which states, 'Ye are godlike beings, and all of you sons of the Most High.']? I have said you are gods … How can you say I blaspheme when I say I am a son of god?" In italics the King James version says, I am "*the*" son of god. However, the earlier Greek version says, I am "a" son of God. Monists or pantheists such as Alan Watts, himself a former priest, understand this in the gnostic sense of all reality, including our own nature, emanating from God but not literally that Jesus is the son of God – any more than you or anyone else is. Christ as a godly begotten son is vehemently rejected by modern atheists (as is made evident by Hitchens) as well as a growing number of Christians.

It is not helpful to simply call things you cannot explain as supernatural or miracles without providing a plausible and logical explanation of how they have meaning or interface with the natural world we have come to know and observe. Although Collins warns us not to use God, miracles, or the supernatural as the cause of explanation for every event or phenomenon we cannot explain, in the end his most extraordinary truths are supported by just that. If God's influences are at play in the universe, then would it not be continuous and comprehensive rather than at key times, as Lewis and Collins seem to suggest? Either all that we observe in reality is miraculous or nothing is. Considering discreteness and plurality has arisen out of uniform singularity, it is all rather miraculous notwithstanding the cause.

George Cunningham weighs Collins' evidence for belief. First, he questions whether the moral law that was so influential in Collin's conversion is uniquely an act of a supernatural, law-giving God. Rather he sees these as "behavioral rules that evolved and are passed on by natural means. The behavioral patterns are those that increase the reproduction and survival of offspring."[257]

Cunningham also culls out problems regarding the term supernatural or at least addressing what we mean by the term supernatural:

> When considering how our natural universe might interact or be affected by the supernatural realm, we need to consider whether there is a different set of supernatural laws that order the spiritual world, however different from natural laws they may be, or whether the supernatural world is chaotic, disorderly and incomprehensible. … Now, if there are some laws, some regularities in the way the supernatural world operates, it should be possible to learn what they are. The supernatural laws could then be integrated into our knowledge of natural laws and expand the area for scientific investigation and explanation.[258]

Cunningham questions how a rational scientist like Collins could ascribe to a personal and perfect God and at the same time a belief in free will. "Let's say we agree with Collins that God uses an evolutionary process to create humans... would God also incorporate the faculty of free will?"[259]

Cunningham also poses the question of evil. If God is good, perfect, how could he permit evil? If suffering is a test, "What new knowledge," he asks, "would an all knowing God learn by testing that God did not previously know?" He then posits a world without free will preferable:

> Would you rather have a world with no suffering, or this world with its burden of misery, injustice, unhappiness, guilt, and free will? Do you prefer this world with free will? Then I guess you prefer this world to heaven, where happiness but not free will is available. If the souls of the departed have free will, they could do evil things in heaven. If they do not have free will, then free will is not essential to human nature.[260]

This is a fair question but may ignore an important component of faith and free will. The trials and tribulations and tough choices we face are not tests for God's knowledge but rather our own. They are a means to temper our spirit, strengthen our faith, and build our character. Knowledge is extremely powerful but can be used to hurt or to heal, to subjugate or free. Thus, it is not what we know that is important but rather what we do, and how we act, given what we know.

It is possible to imagine a supreme and omnipotent being creating humans and all of creation to worship Him singularly without question. But what if instead God created all matter that was dimly aware of this magnificence, responsible no less for their very existence, with the capacity for evolving emerging levels of consciousness. With the potential for ever-growing capacities of reflection and choice and to even behold the stamp of the creator. With the capacity to recognize or ignore that which neither begets nor is begotten, the alpha and the omega. And then to freely choose love, reverence, defiance, arrogance, or indifference. Force of worship would be false worship. But in the end analysis, if God exists, we all will submit willingly or unwillingly. If so, it may be that only those whose will is consistent with that of God should find themselves in any degree of proximity to God or God's heavenly hosts. In such case, all of religions' exhortations to do good and forbid evil become all the more pressing for the soul of man.

In this vein Cunningham rejects Pascal's wager. Blaise Pascal was a 17th century mathematician who specialized in probabilities. He proposed that considering the question of faith and living a morally upright life was a good bet with high stakes. Cunningham summarizes as follows: "If God exists when you die you reap a great benefit-heaven. But if God does not exist Pascal claims you have lost very little. However, if this life is your one and only chance for any sort of happiness or pleasure, you will have sacrificed everything for nothing at all."[261]

Cunningham concludes that "science cannot be harmonized with religious faith. Collins or anyone else can use the tools of science to contribute to our knowledge of the natural world, but they cannot use them to support the theory that god or the supernatural exists."[262]

Metaphysics is that branch of inquiry that seeks to explain what is beyond physics to get to the nature and origin of reality itself. It analyzes the traits manifested by existence of any kind. By definition, it deals with that which is beyond physical or outside objective experience. Anything that is truly outside objective experience and physical existence would be difficult, if not impossible, to understand or detect unless, as Cunningham suggests, it somehow has an effect on the natural or physical world. It may be helpful to direct our attention to not only what is beyond the physical or supernatural but the paraphysical, which consists of that which is beside or alongside what is physical or natural.

If there is God or spirit or immortal souls that are not physical or comprised of matter, then they must have some connection to us – the physical, the natural – to be of any consequence. Indeed, we may come to discover, or have since time immemorial intuitively known, that this all-pervasive, formless, spiritual morass of which no thing exists is the very source that gives life and form to all things.

All monotheistic concepts of God include that which creates but is not created, eternal and supreme, with some kind of power over nature. In this sense we may then develop clues to how this power over nature is exerted, how that power is distributed or realized, but not precisely the nature of that which creates nature (if nature is created at all).

Physicists currently contemplate extra or higher dimensional aspects of space known as hyperspace. String theory has envisioned up to 11 dimensions to explain how subatomic particles are really the result of tiny vibrating strings. Our four-dimensional universe is thought to be restricted to a brane (membrane) in the hyperspace. Other branes in other dimensions can influence our brane and thus introduce effects not typically observed in our standard cosmological models. The four dimensions we observe are length, height, depth, and time. It has been postulated that the fifth dimension, if we could see it, would appear similar but slightly different from our own. In the sixth we would see a plane of possible worlds starting with the same initial conditions as our own beginning with the Big Bang. In the seventh dimension, theoretically, you would be able to envision worlds with different initial conditions than our own and thus with potentially different laws of physics. Beyond the tenth you arrive at the point beyond which nothing further can be imagined or understood.

If string theory and higher dimensions are real and not just useful theories, it would not be unusual to have para-realms existing side by side in direct proximity to our own, even on occasion interacting with our own. Astronomer and mathematician Bernard Carr believes that some of the experiences we have which cannot be explained by our physical laws are because they are occurring in other dimensions. In his book *Matter, Mind and Higher Dimensions*, he writes, "The only non-physical entities in the universe of which we have any experience are mental ones, and … the existence of paranormal phenomena suggests that mental entities have to exist in some sort of space."[263]

Such theories are useful but not fully accepted, particularly for their postulating multiverses which could be interacting with us in countless ways. This would make understanding them of little value to us down here on old-fashioned three- and four-dimensional planet earth in our tiny corner of the universe.

They do provide a means, however, to speculate about other realms such as heaven or hell that might already exist or could come to be in largely inaccessible but nevertheless close proximity to us. They could be as real as the objects in your living room (perhaps even more so) and as close as your own backyard. They could help account for the description of heretofore unexplainable accounts of supernatural entities such as angels, demons, jinn, ghosts, apparitions, and aliens. Of course these same entities could be figments of the imagination, fanciful tales of the past. Or they may be very real physical manifestations that exist in forms and ways we have yet to understand right here in our own physical, four-dimensional universe, operating by laws of physics, mechanics, and presence we have yet to penetrate.

It is virtually inevitable that we will continue to add to our understanding of the universe and all that it contains – and of reality itself, even, where it lies outside the confines of the outer limits of the physical universe. As we do, we close the gaps in our understanding of the splendor of the cosmos and the secrets of its very origin. But we cannot be so arrogant to assume the closing of the gaps will inevitably lead us away from belief in God. Instead it may well lead us to the very gates of Heaven to prostrate in awe at the throne of the Almighty.

Collins does not provide evidentiary support for the deification and resurrection of Jesus, but does in some sense for a plausible theory of theistic evolution (aside from the assumption that

God only performs sporadic acts of supernatural intervention). Cunningham is right to assume any so-called supernatural influences, if having regularity and order, should be discoverable, but is mistaken to summarily conclude that the tools of science cannot be used to support the theory that the supernatural exists. Closing gaps in understanding will narrow the category of the supernatural and broaden the natural. We will surely come to find in all we know, or ever can know, it is both real and natural. That does not mean that God and heaven will not be part of that equation. For now, however, reality is the greatest show in the universe outside of heaven.

CONCLUSION

"I was a Hidden Treasure, and I desired to be known so I created the creatures in order to be known in them."

~ Popular Sufi Saying (often referred to as "the Hadith of the Hidden Treasure")

"My religiosity consists in a humble admiration of the infinitely superior spirit that reveals itself in the little that we, with our weak and transitory understanding, can comprehend of reality. Morality is of the highest importance — but for us, not for God."

~ Albert Einstein

One of the functions of religion is to establish man's place in relationship to God and with each other. It offers an opportunity to adopt a character of virtues, dignity, and humility that atheists often underemphasize. It is true that religion focuses heavily on morals and behavior, but it is folly to suppose it is necessarily at odds with reason or intellect.

Before the advent of modern science, Western society saw advances in science as a means of further explaining God and God's glory. Since the Copernican revolution, Newtonian Physics, and the theory of evolution, society has by-and-large framed science as contrary to this long-standing endeavor, and thereby undermined belief. But these same advances in modern sciences can equally be interpreted to support a higher power, omnipotent being, and natural intelligence. Some of science's brightest minds have so believed and continue to even today.

The Bible talks of a tree of knowledge for which mankind was forever punished for partaking of. In the Quran the tree is not referred to specifically as a tree of knowledge or tree of eternal life. Instead, man is tricked into falsely believing it is a tree of eternal life when in fact it was not. In the Quranic verses, it marks the beginning of God-given moral imperatives, but it also shows even before man slipped and ate from the tree, he already had developed an advanced intellect.

Both Adam and Eve were coerced and freely chose to eat from the tree, even when understanding they were not supposed to. Eve was no more culpable than Adam, and their transgression was not an eternal sin damning all of mankind to hell but rather a slip, a mistake, for which they were almost immediately forgiven. Their choices (like all our ancestors' choices) have incurred consequences that will forever affect us, but they are not, from a moral standpoint, imputed to us. By this religious origin story, neither God nor man are enemies of truth or knowledge, nor is man forbidden from their fruits. Instead, it is a conformation of man's intellect and temporary, transitory abode here on earth, as well as our moral development.

If religion is a poor first attempt at cosmology, then so too is science. How many times have we found old scientific explanations for physical phenomena yield to newer, professedly better, more complete theories? Both science and religion attempt to answer deep questions about us and everything around us, but with a slightly different focus and methodology. Whereas science focuses more on how things came to be, religion focuses more on why things came to be and how they should be. One focuses on the working empirical relationship between objects and things; the other focuses on the meaning and proper interrelationship of these objects and things.

Hitchens in his debate remarked that he could not accept that Jesus dying on the cross was the pivotal and critical event for all of mankind's salvation. Yet his coming and message appears to be foretold by numerous references (as have other prophets and messages). Such predictions imply either fate or foreknowledge (or perhaps luck). If they were indeed fulfilled prophecies, then they suggest divine or metaphysical foresight. Regardless of the means, they serve to reinforce the primacy and importance of the moral law. And not just any law but an objective moral law.

The objective spiritual and moral truths that religion provides allows societies to grow and man to evolve, so that no man is a religion unto himself. Theologians should never banish science, for it is the proof that protects revelations from deviation and their commentary and exegesis from invention. Nor should science suppose that its proofs should ever fulfill the human heart or alone provide meaning from math. Science protects religion from corruption; religion protects society from corruption.

To provide stability and consistency, it is best for moral laws to have longevity and apparent objectivity. If they were easily and frequently changed, they would lose their authority. As Copleston and Russell surmised in their debates, if God does not exist then man has no purpose, other than the purpose he gives himself.

Religion or belief in God provides a purpose for man's existence and hence a framework for objective moral laws that science cannot provide. But belief in God, although rational, particularly from a teleological perspective, is not absolute. Why? Because as Copleston and Russell concluded, most but not all causes are predictable, but whether there is a first cause, at present the best we can come up with is probabilities. However, when we look at the balance and interrelationship between systems, objects, and various substances, there are strong indicators of at least inherent purpose and structure in nature, if not the product of intelligent design.

In the future, statistics are likely to bear this out as we increasingly begin to discover that some form of instruction is embedded throughout nature. The kind of instruction, laws, rules, and parameters that allow physical objects to expand, biological systems to form, and delicate living forms to survive, propagate and evolve. This notwithstanding, you do not need irreducible complexity to prove God exists. Instead, where there is evidence that religion may support not only biological evolution but a much more comprehensive all-pervasive evolution (including abiogenesis and cosmological evolution), it becomes somewhat easier to reconcile science and religion.

If as a theist you do not accept evolution, then it is hard to explain why earlier revelations do not reveal certain physical mysteries that we have only recently come to understand. However, if you accept that the world and we are evolving, then it makes more sense why proclamations ahead of their time might be withheld. Also, although not offered in perfect scientific notation, there are certain religious proclamations that do appear to be fairly accurate, particularly considering our current understanding of physics, biology and the origins of our cosmos. If they fail, it is not in small part due to inaccurate or altered texts as well as frequent misinterpretation.

It is upon questionable texts that our modern atheists descend in exuberant predation. And often for good cause, when most modern biblical scholarship also suspects their authenticity or where the canonical texts are, by their own admission, merely exegesis. Similarly, attacks are made (both fairly and unfairly) upon the institutions, nations, and clergy who have often misappropriated intentionally or unintentionally their teachings. It is for this reason, as Einstein observes, that "fanatical atheists are like slaves who are still feeling the weight of their chains... They are creatures who—in their grudge against traditional religion as the 'opium of the masses'—cannot hear the music of the spheres."[264]

Bertrand Russell was asked on a BBC talk show how he would advise an audience a thousand years from now regarding intellectual and moral matters. He replied, regarding the intellect, that, when "considering any philosophy, ask yourself only what are the facts and what is the truth that the facts bear out. Never let yourself be diverted either by what you wish to believe or by what you think would have beneficent social effects if it were believed, but look only and solely at what are the facts..."[265]

One may concede, by universally accepting and implementing most if not all of the moral guidelines and insights of the world's religions, irrespective of their truth, that many benefits would surely take root. But as Russell warns, you should not blindly accept the dictates of religion, especially if they are contrary to evidence. However, if you elevate science to such an ascendancy – so as to eclipse and negate religion, as it concerns morality, spirituality, sacredness, and meaning – you risk doing humanity and society a disservice. You risk leaving a cold, dark void where mankind needs warmth and light.

Can we then, in our most ardent intellectual inquiries, answer whether or not an omnipotent being or purposeful designer exists? When we begin to explore the true underpinnings of reality, we come to a wall or threshold of which it is hard to cross. As Dennett has concluded, we run into a timeless possibility of what appears to be a mindless, valueless algorithmic process. In the end we cannot come to a decisive conclusion on this eternal and epic debate – at least not by scientific proofs, it seems. Nor by such proofs can we find with empirical certainty the "one true religion." In the end, the only true religion is the one you cultivate in your heart from the field of all experience.

But by looking at the historical landscape, the academic scholarship, the current sciences, we see the contours of the limits we run into in attempting to find our answer. By looking carefully at the religious and scientific landscape, we find our best efforts and results in documenting what we believe to be objective truths.

Should we be surprised at the number and variety of scientific contributions of the medieval Iraqi Muslim physicist Alhazen? He made great advancements in the fields of optics, astronomy, medicine, mathematics and physics, and is generally credited with the introduction of the scientific method. He is described by some Western authors as the first scientist and first experimentational psychologist. Alhazen believed that faith should be reserved to God and his prophets, not to any other authorities such as mathematicians or specialists in the demonstrative sciences.

He, similarly to Russell, advises that "the duty of the man who investigates the writings of scientists, if learning the truth is his goal, is to make himself an enemy of all that he reads, and, applying his mind to the core and margins of its content, attack it from every side. He should also suspect himself as he performs his critical examination of it, so that he may avoid falling into either prejudice or leniency." But he also admits, "I constantly sought knowledge and truth, and it became my belief that for gaining access to the effulgence and closeness to God, there is no better way than that of searching for truth and knowledge."[266]

Mankind has this constant driving desire to know, to seek, to understand evermore. But can we ever expect to understand it all, to form the right cosmology or philosophy? Even though we can have theories of everything, we cannot have a unified knowledge or consciousness of everything. The only concept of a being that can know and detect everything that ever was or ever could be known and detected, is that of a supreme, omniscient being.

When inquiring of the existence of an omnipotent and intelligent designer we should consider the possibility that, by virtue of the creator's elevated position, we are not on the same plane of existence. We must allow for the possibility that the reason that the connection between us and the exalted is not more blatant is one of both necessity and design. We may forever find ourselves floundering at a barrier that has been pre-imposed and yet we do not have forever. We only have the here and now, and a very limited amount of time.

When we begin to comprehend the source of all that our eyes and ears and every sensory perception is able to perceive (which in turn produced within us every emotion ever evoked) may be coming from and generated from a single source, only then may we begin to appreciate the truly awesome, magnificent and sheer power of the one supreme omnipotence. Only then do we come to understand our own relative humble humility and, at the same time, our special place in having been given the opportunity to gaze upon the splendor – nay, yet more, to be immersed within it and to help fulfill its existence.

BIBLIOGRAPHY

Akbar, Arifa. "Mao's Great Leap Forward 'killed 45 million in four years.'" *The Independent*, 17 Sep. 2010, https://www.independent.co.uk/arts-entertainment/books/news/maos-great-leap-forward-killed-45-million-in-four-years-2081630.html. Accessed 11 Sep. 2023.

Alfred, Jay. "Jinns - Plasma Aliens from a Parallel Earth." *Unexplained Mysteries*, 14 July 2008, https://www.unexplained-mysteries.com/column.php?id=130606. Accessed 20 July 2023.

Alakbarli, Farid. "A 13th-Century Darwin? - Tusi's Views on Evolution" *Azer.com*, 2001, azer.com/aiweb/categories/magazine/92_folder/92_articles/92_tusi.html. Accessed 10 Jan. 2022.

Al-Zuhili, Wahebeh. *Islam and International Law*. Int'l Rev. Red Cross, June 2005.

ANU Staff. "Earth Was Barren, Mountainless and Almost Entirely under Water 4.4 Billion Years Ago – ANU Study." *Australian National University*, 9 May 2017, https://www.anu.edu.au/news/all-news/earth-was-barren-mountainless-and-almost-entirely-under-water-44-billion-years-ago-%E2%80%93. Accessed 19 July 2023.

"Are We Looking for Aliens in the Wrong Places?" *HowStuffWorks*, 20 Aug. 2007, science.howstuffworks.com/weird-life.htm. Accessed 10 Jan. 2022.

Arkoun, Mohammed. *Lectures Du Coran*. Tunis, Alif- Éd. De La Méditerranée, 1991.

Armstrong, Karen. *Fields of Blood: Religion and the History of Violence*. Anchor, 2015.

___. *The Case for God*. Toronto, Vintage Canada, 2010.

Aslan, Reza. *Zealot*. Random House, 2014.

Ashworth, William B. Jr. "Scientist of the day - Albert Einstein." Linda Hall Library, 18 Apr. 2023, https://www.lindahall.org/about/news/scientist-of-the-day/albert-einstein-2. Accessed 11 Sep. 2023.

Bar-Ron, Michael S. "The Seal of Joseph." *Beth Midrash Ohel Moshe*, 29 Dec. 2017, https://www.academia.edu/35532146/The_Seal_of_Joseph_in_His_Palace_at_Tell_Ed_Daba_Re_edited. Accessed 10 Jan. 2022.

Barnes, Jonathan, translator. *Early Greek Philosophy*. Penguin Classics, 2002.

Bauckham, Richard. *Jesus and the Eyewitnesses : The Gospels as Eyewitness Testimony*. Eerdmans, 2006.

"BBC - Religions - Judaism: Joseph." *Bbc.co.uk*, 2009, www.bbc.co.uk/religion/religions/judaism/history/joseph.shtml.

BBC Staff. (2012, July 20). "Muslims in Burma's Rakhine state 'abused' - Amnesty." *BBC News*. https://www.bbc.com/news/world-asia-18921960

Becker, Kate. "Is Information Fundamental?" *PBS*, 25 Apr. 2014, https://www.pbs.org/wgbh/nova/article/is-information-fundamental/. Accessed 16 Sep. 2023.

Blaxland, Beth & Fran Dorey. "Larger brains." *Australian Museum*, 2 Nov. 2018, https://australian.museum/learn/science/human-evolution/larger-brains/. Accessed 18 Sep. 2023.

Branch, Glenn. "'Harun Yahya' sentenced to over 8500 years." NCSE: National Center for Science Education, 22 Nov. 2022, https://ncse.ngo/harun-yahya-sentenced-over-8500-years. Accessed 24 Sep. 2023.

Britt, Robert Roy. "Unlikely Cousins: Whales and Hippos." *Live Science*, 25 Jan. 2004.

Byrnes, Sholto. "*The Rage Against God, By Peter Hitchens.*" *The Independent*, London. Archived from the original on 12 May 2010.

Cadbury Research Library Staff. "Birmingham Qur'an Manuscript Dated among the Oldest in the World." *University of Birmingham*, 22 July 2015, https://www.birmingham.ac.uk/news-archive/2015/birmingham-quran-manuscript-dated-among-the-oldest-in-the-world. Accessed 18 July 2023.

Caltech Faculty. "What Is the Uncertainty Principle and Why Is It Important?" *Caltech Science Exchange*, https://scienceexchange.caltech.edu/topics/quantum-science-explained/uncertainty-principle. Accessed 18 Sep. 2023.

Cain, Fraser. "When was the first light in the universe?" *Phys.org*, 7 Nov. 2016, https://phys.org/news/2016-11-universe.html. Accessed 21 Sep. 2023.

Chotiner, Isaac. "Interview: Richard Dawkins Keeps Making New Enemies." *The New Republic*, 28 Oct. 2013, https://newrepublic.com/article/115339/richard-dawkins-interview-archbishop-atheism. Accessed 24 June 2023.

Clark, Ronald William. *Einstein: The Life and Times*. London, Bloomsbury Reader, 2013.

Cleeves, L. I., et al. "The Ancient Heritage of Water Ice in the Solar System." *Science*, vol. 345, no. 6204, 25 Sep. 2014, pp. 1590–1593, 10.1126/science.1258055.

Collins, Francis. *The Language of God*. Free Press, 2006.

Cooper, John. "Mulla Sadra." *Muslim Philosophy*, https://www.muslimphilosophy.com/ip/rep/H027.htm. Accessed 19 June 2023.

Coughlan, Sean. "'Oldest' Koran Found in Birmingham." *BBC News*,22July2015,www.bbc.com/news/business-33436021.

Cunningham, George C. *Decoding the Language of God: Can a Scientist Really Be a Believer? A Geneticist Responds to Francis Collins*. Amherst, N.Y., Prometheus Books, 2010.

"Dark Energy, Dark Matter." *NASA Science*, https://science.nasa.gov/astrophysics/focus-areas/what-is-dark-energy#:~:text=It%20turns%20out%20that%20roughly,than%205%25%20of%20the%20universe. Accessed 18 Sep. 2023.

Darwin, Charles. *On the Origin of Species*. 1859. S.L., Alma Classics, 2019.

Dawkins, Richard. *The God Delusion*. London Black Swan, 2006.

Dennett III, Daniel C. *Darwin's Dangerous Ideas*. Simon and Schuster, 1996.

de Spinoza, Benedictus. *Tractatus Theologico-politicus*. Translated by Robert Willis. Trübner & Company, 1868.

Devlin, Hannah. "Maximum human lifespan could far exceed 115 years - new research," *The Guardian*, 28 June 2017, https://www.theguardian.com/science/2017/jun/28/maximum-human-lifespan-new-research-mortality. Accessed 6 Sep. 2023.

"Earth: Egg-Shaped." *Quran Talk Blog*, 1 July 2020, https://qurantalkblog.com/2020/07/01/earth-egg-shaped/. Accessed 19 Sep. 2023.

Editors of Canterbury Classics. *Ancient Greek Philosophers*. Canterbury Classics, 2018.

Elsheik, Elsheikh M. "Evolution Physical Intelligent Guiding Principle." *Energy, Ecology and Environment*, vol. 1, no. 2, 14 Feb. 2016, pp. 75–85, 10.1007/s40974-016-0010-2. Accessed 10 May 2020.

Emeritus, Robert, and Gregory Alles, editors. *The Encyclopedia of World Religions*. Facts on File, 2007.

European Commission. *Eurobarometer Report on Biotechnology*. 15 Dec. 2010.

Eve, Eric. *Behind the Gospels: Understanding the Oral Tradition*. Minneapolis, Fortress Press, 2014.

Fassler, Joe. "The Book That Changed Reza Aslan's Mind about Jesus." *The Atlantic*, 6 Aug. 2013, www.theatlantic.com/entertainment/archive/2013/08/the-book-that-changed-reza-aslans-mind-about-jesus/278410/. Accessed 10 Jan. 2022.

Finkelstein, Israel, and Neil Silberman. *The Bible Unearthed: Archaeology's New Vision of Ancient Israel and the Origin of Its Sacred Texts*. Simon and Schuster, 2001.

Foch, Marshal. "Of the Commercial Interests That Lead to War," *United Service Magazine*. pp. 212 no. 1081, Dec. 1918.

"Fr. Copleston vs. Bertrand Russell: The Famous 1948 BBC Radio Debate on the Existence of God." *Biblicalcatholic.com*, www.biblicalcatholic.com/apologetics/p20.htm.

"Gallup International Religiosity Index" (PDF). *Washington Post*. WIN-Gallup International. April 2015.

Ġazālī Al-, and Bankey Behari. *The Revival of Religious Sciences*. Farnham, Surrey, Sufi Publishing Co, 1972.

George Sylvester Viereck. *Glimpses of the Great*. London, Duckworth, 1930.

Ghosh, Pallab. *Earliest evidence of life on earth found*, BBC News Science, March 1, 2017.

"God - CTMU Wiki." *Ctmucommunity.org*, ctmucommunity.org/wiki/God. Accessed 10 Jan. 2022.

Gosh, Pallab. "Earliest Evidence of Life on Earth Found." *BBC News Science*, 1 Mar. 2017.

Gould, Stephen J. "Impeaching a Self Appointed Judge." *Scientific American*.

Halsall, Paul, editor. "Munkidh Min Al-Dalal (Deliverance from Error)." *Ghazali*, https://www.ghazali.org/books/md/gz101.htm. Accessed 29 Apr. 2023.

Handwerk, Brian. "An Evolutionary Timeline of Homo Sapiens." *Smithsonian Magazine*, 2 Feb. 2021.

Harpur, Tom. *The Pagan Christ: Recovering the Lost Light.* Toronto, Ont., Thomas Allen Publishers, 2004.

Harris, Sam. *The End of Faith: Religion, Terror, and the Future of Reason.* London, Free Press, 2006.

Hayward, Joel. *Warfare in the Qur'an* . MABDA, 2012.

Hecht, Jennifer Michael. *Doubt: A History.* New York, HarperCollins, 2004.

Henson, Daniel. "Dossier of Reason." *Google Docs*, docs.google.com/document/d/1f6ZewV_Ro5HLixACGE_wgJrnlFNVKVxTfuVALqARNEs/edit?pli=1&hl=en_US#. Accessed 10 Jan. 2022.

Himma, Kenneth E. "Design Arguments for the Existence of God." *Internet Encyclopedia of Philosophy*, 10 Sep. 2023, https://iep.utm.edu/design-arguments-for-existence-of-god/#SH1b.

Hirai, Hisashi. "[Research Report] 'Comrade Kim Jong-un›s revolutionary thought.'" The Japan Institute of International Affairs, 20 Feb. 2023, https://www.jiia.or.jp/en/column/2023/02/korean-peninsula-fy2022-01.html. Accessed 16 Sep. 2023.

Hitchens, Christopher. *God Is Not Great: How Religion Poisons Everything.* Twelve, 2007.

Hitchens, Peter. *Rage against God.* S.L., Bloomsbury Continuum, 2019.

Horsley, Richard A, and Jonathan A Draper. *Whoever Hears You Hears Me: Prophets, Performance, and Tradition in Q.* Harrisburg Pa., Trinity Press International, 1999.

Hussain, Irshaad. "The Water of Creation." *Islam from Inside*, 16 Feb. 2013, http://www.islamfrominside.com/Pages/Tafsir/The_water_of_creation.html. Accessed 20 Feb. 2023.

Ibn Al-Haytham- Alhazen. *Al-Shukūk 'alā Batlamyūs (Doubts concerning Ptolemy)*, 1028 C.E.

Ibn Khaldūn, et al. *An Introduction to History: The Muqaddimah.* London, Routledge and Kegan Paul In Association With Secker And Warburg, 1967.

Iqbal, Muhammad. *The Reconstruction of Religious Thought in Islam.* Lahore, Iqbal Academy Pakistan, 2011.

Irwin, Klee. "The Code-Theoretic Axiom: The Third Ontology." *Reports in Advances of Physical Sciences*, vol. 03, no. 01, Mar. 2019, p. 1950002, 10.1142/s2424942419500026. Accessed 10 Jan. 2022.

Isaacson, Walter. *Einstein: His Life and Universe.* New York, Simon & Schuster Paperbacks, 2017.

Islam, Joseph. "Adam (pbuh) an Earthly Abode or Paradise?" *Quranmessage.com*, 2010.

James, Albert. "Science and God, Dialogue with Einstein." *Forum and Century 83*, June 1930.

Jalajel, David S. *Islam and Biological Evolution: Exploring Classical Sources and Methodologies.* Bellville, University Of The Western Cape, 2009.

Jordan, Gary, host. "Apollo 8: Part 1." *Houston We Have a Podcast*, 21 Dec. 2018, https://www.nasa.gov/johnson/HWHAP/apollo-8-part-1. Accessed 6 Sep. 2023.

Judd, E E, and A P Warren. *Why War Is Near; Conflicting Capitalist Interests.* Sydney, Socialist Labor Party Of Australia, 1931.

Kalin, Ibrahim. "Sadr al-Din Shirazi (Mulla Sadra) (b. 1571-1640)," in Iqbal, Muzaffar; Kalin, Ibrahim, *Resources on Islam & Science*, March 2001.

"Keats' Letters." *British Literature Wiki*, https://sites.udel.edu/britlitwiki/preliminary-keats-letters-page/. Accessed 16 Sep. 2023.

Keller, Evelyn Fox. "A Clash of Two Cultures." *Nature*, 2002.

Keller, Nun Ha Mim. "Islam and Evolution a Letter to Suleman Ali." *Masud*, 14 July 1995, http://www.masud.co.uk/ISLAM/nuh/evolve.htm. Accessed 19 July 2023.

Kessler, Edward. *What Do Jews Believe?: The Customs and Culture of Modern Judaism*. New York, Walker & Company, 2007.

Klug, Foster. "Juche rules North Korean propaganda, but what does it mean?" *Associated Press*, 29 Sep. 2019, https://apnews.com/general-news-d63d00ce9de042dc88b9df2c40be53ee. Accessed 16 Sep. 2023.

Kolko, Gabriel. *The Politics of War: The World and United States Foreign Policy, 1943-1945*. New York, Pantheon Books, 1990.

Lacey, Robert. *History of Saudi Arabia from 1979 to Date*, 2009.

Langan, Christopher. "The Cognitive-Theoretic Model of the Universe:A New Kind of Reality Theory." *Semantic Scholar*, https://www.semanticscholar.org/paper/The-Cognitive-Theoretic-Model-of-the-Universe%3A-A-of-Langan/537ac9c6066f20039491a72b361a4009a3d5623f. Accessed 19 June 2023.

Leshem, Ayval. *Newton on Mathematics and Spiritual Purity*. Dordrecht; Boston, Kluwer Academic Publishers, 2003.

Lewis, C. S. *Mere Christianity*. 1952. Glasgow, Fount Paperbacks, 1977.

___. *Miracles: A Preliminary Study*. London, Collins, 1960.

Lincoln, Don. "The Good Vibrations of Quantum Field Theories." *PBS*, 5 Aug. 2013, https://www.pbs.org/wgbh/nova/article/the-good-vibrations-of-quantum-field-theories/. Accessed 18 Sep. 2023.

Lipka, Michael. "10 facts about atheists." *Pew Research Center*, 6 Dec. 2019, https://www.pewresearch.org/short-reads/2019/12/06/10-facts-about-atheists/. Accessed 8 Aug. 2023.

Lucas, Jim. "What are gamma rays?" *Live Science*, 29 Nov. 2018, https://www.livescience.com/50215-gamma-rays.html#:~:text=Gamma%20rays%20have%20frequencies%20greater,it%20hard%20to%20differentiate%20them. Accessed 18 Sep. 2023.

___. "What is visible light?" *Live Science*, 23 May 2022, https://www.livescience.com/50678-visible-light.html. Accessed 18 Sep. 2023.

MacIsaac, Tara. "Astronomer Says Spiritual Phenomena Exist in Other Dimensions." *The Epoch Times*, 7 Apr. 2014, https://www.theepochtimes.com/astronomer-says-spiritual-phenomena-exist-in-other-dimensions_605634.html?welcomeuser=1. Accessed 20 June 2023.

"Mao's Marginal Notes to Friedrich Paulsen, a System of Ethics," *Mao Zedong Zaoqi Wengao (Early Manuscripts of Mao Zedong)*. CCP Archive Study Office And CCP Hunan Committee, eds. Changsha: Hunan Chubanshe, 1990.

Marshall, Perry. "'If You Can Read This Sentence, I Can Prove God Exists.'" *Evolution 2.0*, 26 May 2009, https://evo2.org/prove-god-exists/. Accessed 19 June 2023.

Marx, Karl. *A Contribution to the Critique of Hegel's Philosophy of Right*, Feb. 1844. Edited by Andy Blunden, https://www.marxists.org/archive/marx/works/1843/critique-hpr/intro.htm. Accessed 11 Sep. 2023.

Masood, Ehsan. *Science and Islam: A History.* Icon Books, 2017.

McCray, Richard. "7. Evolution of the Milky Way." *Jila.colorado.edu*, 3 March 2002, https://jila.colorado.edu/~ajsh/courses/astr1120_03/text/chapter8/l8S7.htm. Accessed 21 Sep. 2023.

Mcrae, Mike. "Scientists Just Found a Vital Missing Link in The Origins of Life on Earth." *Science Alert*, 7 Nov. 2017, https://www.sciencealert.com/compound-explains-phosphorylation-mystery-abiogenesis-origins-life. Accessed 19 July 2023.

Miles, Leroyce. *Introduction to the Study of Religion.* Ed Tech Press, 2018.

Miller, David Ian. "FINDING MY RELIGION / Religious scholar Elaine Pagels on how the newly discovered Gospel of Judas sheds new light on the dawn of Christianity." *SFGATE*, 2 Apr. 2007, https://www.sfgate.com/news/article/FINDING-

MY-RELIGION-Religious-scholar-Elaine-2605086.php. Accessed 16 Sep. 2023.

Muhammad B Muhammad Abu Hamid Al-Gazali, et al. *Deliverance from Error and Mystical Union with the Almighty (Al-Mungidh Min Al-Dalal)*. Washington, The Council For Research In Values And Philosophy, 2001.

Muhammad Hamidullah, et al. *The Emergence of Islam: Bahawalpur Lectures on the Development of Islamic World-View, Intellectual Tradition and Polity*. Islamabad, Islamic Research Institute, 2010.

Musser, George. "What Einstein Really Thought about Quantum Mechanics." *Scientific American*, 1 Sep. 2015, https://www.scientificamerican.com/article/what-einstein-really-thought-about-quantum-mechanics/. Accessed 11 Sep. 2023.

NASA Staff. "The Star Splitters: The Mystery of the Missing Mass," *NASA*, https://history.nasa.gov/SP-466/ch22.htm- mystery of the missing mass. Accessed 21 Feb. 2023.

___. "Will the Universe Expand Forever?" *NASA*, 24 Jan. 2014, https://map.gsfc.nasa.gov/universe/uni_shape.html. Accessed 20 Feb. 2023.

Newman, Hugh. "Top Ten Giant Discoveries in North America." *Ancient Origins*, 12 Feb. 2022, https://www.ancient-origins.net/unexplained-phenomena/giants-north-america-005196. Accessed 15 Sep. 2023.

Pagels, Elaine & King, Karen L. *Reading Judas: The Gospel of Judas and the Shaping of Christianity*. New York: Viking Adult, 2007. ISBN 978-0670038459.

Paley, William. *Natural Theology or Evidences of the Existence and Attributes of the Deity*. R. Faulder, 1802.

Peratt, Anthony L. "Electric space: Evolution of the plasma universe." Astrophysics and Space Science, March 1996, Volume 244, Issue 1-2, pp. 89-103. DOI: 10.1007/BF00642283.

PEW Staff. "Muslim Publics Share Concerns about Extremist Groups." *Pew Research Center (PEW)*, 10 Sep. 2013, https://www.pewresearch.org/global/2013/09/10/muslim-publics-share-concerns-about-extremist-groups/.

Pirsig, Robert M. *Lila: An Inquiry into Morals*. Bantam Books, 1992.

___. *Zen and the Art of Motorcycle Maintenance*. New York, Bantam Books, 1974.

Pospielovsky, Dimitry, V. *A History of Soviet Atheism in Theory and Practice, and the Believer. 2. Soviet Antireligious Campaigns and Persecutions. - 1. Publ. - 1988. - XIX, 275 S.* Basingstoke U.A., Macmillan, 1988.

Rackham, H., translator. *Aristotle in 23 Volumes*, Vol. 19. Cambridge, MA, Harvard University Press; London, William Heinemann Ltd., 1934.

Ramadan, Tariq. *Radical Reform: Islamic Ethics and Liberation*. Oxford; New York, Oxford University Press, 2009.

Rand, Ayn, *Philosophy and a Sense of Life*, World Publishing Company, 1970.

___, *Philosophy, Who Needs It: Essays*. Indianapolis, Bobbs-Merrill, 1982.

___. *The Romantic Manifesto*. New York, New American Library, 1975.

___. *Ayn Rand Letter 1971-1976*. Ayn Rand Institute, 2021.

Ratner, Joseph. "George Santayana's Theory of Religion." *The Journal of Religion*, vol. 3, no. 5, Sep. 1923, pp. 458–475, 10.1086/480381. Accessed 19 Nov. 2020.

"Religiosity and Atheism Index." (PDF). Zurich: *WIN/GIA*, 27 July 2012, http://www.wingia.com/web/files/news/14/file/14.pdf. Accessed 1 Oct 2013.

Sadeghi, Behnam, & Moshen Goudarzi. *Sana 1 and the Origins of the Qur'an*. Der Islam, 2012.

Sadeghi, Behnam & Uwe Bergmann. "The Codex of a Companion of the Prophet and the Qurān of the Prophet." *Arabica* 57, 343-436, 2010. 10.1163/157005810X504518.

Samuel Enoch Stumpf, and James Fieser. *Socrates to Sartre and beyond: A History of Philosophy*. New York, Mcgraw-Hill, 2008.

Science. "Human Mortality at Extreme Age," *Science*, 29 Jun. 2018, https://www.sciencemagazinedigital.org/sciencemagazine/29_june_2018/MobilePagedReplica.action?pm=2&folio=Cover#. Accessed 19 Nov. 2020.

"Science Magazine - June 29, 2018 - Page1." *SMD,* www.sciencemagazinedigital.org/sciencemagazine/29_june_2018. Accessed 10 Jan. 2022.

Shah, Niaz A. "The Use of Force under Islamic Law." European Journal of International Law, Volume 24, Issue 1, February 2013, 1 April 2013, https://doi.org/10.1093/ejil/cht013.

Shankland, Stephen. "Neil DeGrasse Tyson: US Need Not Lose Its Edge in Science ." *CNET*, 20 June 2014, https://www.cnet.com/science/neil-degrasse-tyson-the-us-doesnt-have-to-lose-its-edge-in-science/. Accessed 29 Apr. 2023.

Sharan, Shankar. "Fifty Different Tellings of the Quran." *Indiafacts.org*, 2015, https://indiafacts.org/fifty-different-tellings-of-the-quran/. Accessed 11 Sep. 2023.

Shermer, Michael. "Science, Religion and the Meaning of Life." *Scientific American*, 2015, https://www.scientificamerican.com/article/science-religion-and-the-meaning-of-life/. Accessed 23 Aug. 2023.

Smith, Huston. *The World's Great Religions*. 1958. San Francisco, Harper, 1991.

___. *The World's Religions*. HarperOne, 2009.

Smith, Morgan. "Cosmic Oceans: The Primordial Waters of Ancient Creation Myths." *Ancient Origins*, 28 July 2019, https://www.ancient-origins.net/human-origins/primordial-waters-0012363. Accessed 1 July 2023.

"Social values, Science and Technology." Directorate General Research, European Union, Special Eurobarometer 225, June 2005, https://web.archive.org/web/20110430163128/http://ec.europa.eu/public_opinion/archives/ebs/ebs_225_report_en.pdf. Accessed 11 Sep. 2023.

Spinoza, Baruch. *The Ethics.* 1677. Translated by William White, 1883.

Stille, Alexander. "Scholars Are Quietly Offering New Theories of the Koran." *The New York Times*, 2 Mar. 2022, https://www.nytimes.com/2002/03/02/arts/scholars-are-quietly-offering-new-theories-of-the-koran.html. Accessed 20 June 2023.

Stumpf, Samuel E. *Socrates to Sartre: A History of Philosophy*. McGraw-Hill, 1975.

Sultan Shah, Muhammad. *Pre-Darwinian Muslim Scholars' Views on Evolution*. pu.edu.pk/images/journal/uoc/PDF-FILES/(11)%20Dr.%20Sultan%20Shah_86_2.pdf.

Taher, Abul. "Querying the Koran." *The Guardian*, 8 Aug. 2000, https://www.theguardian.com/education/2000/aug/08/highereducation.theguardian. Accessed 20 May 2023.

"THE CASE against HENRY KISSINGER." *Harpers Magazine*, Feb. 2001.

Thompson, LG, et al. "Kilimanjaro ice core records: evidence of holocene climate change in tropical Africa." *Science*, 18 Oct 2002. 298(5593):589-93. doi: 10.1126/science.1073198. PMID: 12386332.

Tietke, Mathias. *Yoga in Der DDR: Geächtet, Geduldet, Gefördert.* Kiel, Ludwig, 2014.

____. *Yoga im Nationalsozialismus: Konzepte, Kontraste, Konsequenzen.* Ludwig; 1st edition, 16 Sep. 2011.

Tompkins, Ptolemy. *Proof of God.* Howard Books, 2017.

Townsend, Peggy. "Did Life Begin ... on Land?" *University of California*, 19 July 2017, https://www.universityofcalifornia.edu/news/did-life-begin-land. Accessed 19 July 2023.

Trefil, James. "Evidence for a Flood." *Smithsonian Magazine*, www.smithsonianmag.com/science-nature/evidence-for-a-flood-102813115/#bKTk5srLeIccies3.99. Accessed 10 Jan. 2022.

Turner, Louis. "The Seven Sisters: The Great Oil Companies and the World They Made, the New Oil Stakes, Oil and Politics, Oil: A Plain Man's Guide to the World's Energy Crisis and the Oil Security System: An Import Strategy for Achieving Oil Security and Reducing Oil Prices." *International Affairs*, vol. 52, no. 1, Jan. 1976, pp. 96–99, 10.2307/2616091. Accessed 22 Apr. 2020.

Walker, John. *Did a Historical Jesus Exist? Nobeliefs.com*, 12 June 1997, https://www.nobeliefs.com/exist.htm.

Watts, Alan. "Out of Your Mind 01: The Nature of Consciousness (Part 1)." *The Library*, www.organism.earth/library/document/16. Accessed 10 Jan. 2022.

Westphal, Jonathan. "Descartes and the Discovery of the Mind-Body Problem." *The MIT Press Reader*, 8 Aug. 2019, https://thereader.mitpress.mit.edu/discovery-mind-body-problem/. Accessed 18 Sep. 2023.

Wheeler, John Archibald. "Information, physics, quantum: the search for links." *Proceedings III International Symposium on Foundations of Quantum Mechanics*, 1989. Tokyo: pp. 354-358.

William, John. *History of the Conflict between Religion and Science. (Republished).* 1874. Farnborough, Hants.: Gregg International Publishers, 1970.

Williams, Matt. "What is the Big Bang Theory?" *Phys.org*, 18 Dec 2015, https://phys.org/news/2015-12-big-theory.html. Accessed 18 Sep. 2023.

Yahya, Harun. *Tell Me about the Creation*. New Delhi, Goodword Books, Repr, 2003.

Zinn, Howard. *A People's History of the United States*. Harper, 1980.

Online Videos

"1.2.7. - Eco Zen - Pt. 1." *Alan Watts Organization*, 16 Apr. 2019, www.alanwatts.org/searchable/1-2-7-eco-zen-pt-1/. Accessed 10 Jan. 2022.

"Alan Watts Eco Zen." *YouTube*, uploaded by Uriah Lathrop, 9 Jun. 2023, www.youtube.com/watch?v=9ZFDPLeZArw.

"Bertrand Russell." *BBC*, uploaded by Face to Face, 13 Nov. 1988, www.bbc.co.uk/programmes/p04qgxlv.

"God Is Not a Good Theory (Sean Carroll)." *YouTube*, uploaded by PhilosophyCosmology, 5 Jun. 2013, https://www.youtube.com/watch?v=ew_cNONhhKI

"Purpose and the Universe by Sean M. Carroll, Ph.D (with HD Slides) at the 2013 AHA Conference." *www.youtube.com*, www.youtube.com/watch?v=bcqd3Q7X_1A. Accessed 10 Jan. 2022.

"Religion and Reason Debate | C-SPAN.org." *c-Span.org*, 25 Jan. 2007, www.c-span.org/video/?196385-1.

"The God Debate: Hitchens Vs. D'Souza." *YouTube*, uploaded by University of Notre Dame,

22 Apr. 2010, www.youtube.com/watch?v=9V85OykSDT8.

"The Moon, the Tides and Why Neil DeGrasse Tyson Is Colbert's God." *The Science Network*, 20 Jan. 2011, thesciencenetwork.org/programs/the-science-studio/neil-degrasse-tyson-2.

Qur'an Citations

Various English Translations

Hadith Citations

Sahih al-Albani

Sahih al-Bukhari

Sahih Muslim

Sunan al-Tirmidhi

Sunan Abu Dawood

Sunan Ibn Maajah

Bible Citations

Various English Translations

Endnotes

1 See, for instance, Michael Lipka, "10 facts about atheists," 2019.

2 For definitions and details on certain religious and/or spiritual terms,See Robert Emeritus and Gregory Alles, *The Encyclopedia of World Religions*, 2007.

3 See, for instance, Karen Armstrong, *Fields of Blood: Religion and the History of Violence*, 2015.

4 See, for instance, Huston Smith, *The World's Religions*, 2009.

5 See Charles Darwin, *On the Origin of Species*, 1859.

6 See, for instance, Jonathan Barnes, translator, *Early Greek Philosophy*, 2002; editors of Canterbury Classics, *Ancient Greek Philosophers*, 2018.

7 See "God Is Not a Good Theory (Sean Carroll)." 5 June, 2013. This is a lecture from the 2nd miniseries (Is 'God' Explanatory) from the "Philosophy of Cosmology" project; a University of Oxford and Cambridge Collaboration.

8 Ibid. "...governments should derive their power from the consent of the governed" is a reference to the U.S. Declaration of Independence.

9 See "The Moon, the Tides and Why Neil DeGrasse Tyson Is Colbert›s God," 20 Jan. 2011.

10 See Stephen Shankland, "Neil DeGrasse Tyson: US Need Not Lose Its Edge in Science," 20 June 2014.

11 See, for instance, Muhammad al-Ghazali's *Ihya Ulum Ad-din (Revival of Religious Sciences).*

12 See Paul Halsall, editor, "Munkidh Min Al-Dalal (Deliverance from Error)," ca. 1100.

13 See, for instance, Ehsan Masood, *Science and Islam: A History*, 2017.

14 See Kenneth Himma, "Design Arguments for the Existence of God," IEP. Accessed 10 Sep. 2023.

15 JWV Huyssteen, editor. *Encyclopedia of Science and Religion*, 2003, 621.

16 Ayval Leshem, *Newton on Mathematics and Spiritual Purity*, 2003, p. 20.

17 Ibid.

18 See William Paley, *Natural Theology or Evidences of the Existence and Attributes of the Deity,* 1802.

19 See Charles Darwin, *On the Origin of Species*, 1859, p. 189.

20 Ayn Rand, *Philosophy and a Sense of Life*, 1970, p. 32.

21 Ibid., p. 38.

22 Ayn Rand, *Ayn Rand Letter 1971-1976*, 2021.

23 Ibid.

24 Ayn Rand, *Philosophy: Who Needs it?* 1982, p. 6.

25 Ibid., p. 8.

26 Ibid., p. 26.

27 Ibid., p. 92.

28 Ayn Rand, *Romantic Manifesto,* 1971, p. 52.

29 See Brandon Vogt, "The Most Famous Debate on the Existence of God." Accessed 20 Apr. 2023.

30 Samuel Stumpf, *Socrates to Sartre, A History of Philosophy,* 1975, p. 267.

31 See Brandon Vogt, "The Most Famous Debate on the Existence of God." Accessed 20 Apr. 2023.

32 Ibid.

33 Ibid.

34 See "The God Debate: Hitchens Vs. D›Souza." *YouTube*, 22 Apr. 2010.

35 See "The God Debate: Hitchens Vs. D›Souza." *YouTube*, 22 Apr. 2010.

36 See Gallup International Religiosity Index, *Washington Post*, April 2015; "Social values, Science and Technology." Directorate General Research, European Union, June 2005.

37 See "Religiosity and Atheism Index," WIN/GIA, 27 July 2012.

38 Christopher Hitchens, *God is not Great*, 2007, p. 4.

39 Ibid. Chapter 7.

40 Ibid. Chapter 8.

41 For definitions and details on certain religious and/or spiritual terms,See Robert Emeritus, and Gregory Alles, *The Encyclopedia of World Religions*, 2007.

42 See Christipher Hitchens, *God is not Great, 2007*; Chapter 9.

43 Ibid., p. 236.

44 See European Commission, *Eurobarometer Report on Biotechnology*, 15 Dec. 2010.

45 Karl Marx. *A Contribution to the Critique of Hegel›s Philosophy of Right*, Feb. 1844.

46 Dimitry Pospielovsky, *A History of Soviet Atheism in Theory, and Practice, and the Believer, vol 2: Soviet Antireligous Campaigns and Persecutions*, 1988.

47 "*Marginal notes to Friedrich Paulsen, A System of Ethics*," Mao Zedong zaoqi wengao (Early Manuscripts of Mao Zedong), CCP Archive Study Office And CCP Hunan Committee, eds., 1990, pp. 116-275.

48 Arifa Akbar, "Mao's Great Leap Forward 'killed 45 million in four years," 17 Sep. 2010.

49 See Marshal Foch, "Of the Commercial Interests That Lead to War," *United Service Magazine*, no. 1081 p. 212, Dec. 1918.

50 Sholto Byrnes, "*The Rage Against God, By Peter Hitchens,*" 7 May, 2010.

51 Hisashi Hirai, "[Research Report] 'Comrade Kim Jong-un›s revolutionary thought.'" The Japan Institute of International Affairs, 20 Feb. 2023.

52 Foster Klug, "Juche rules North Korean propaganda, but what does it mean?", Associated Press, 29 Sep. 2019.

53 Sholto Byrnes, "*The Rage Against God, By Peter Hitchens,*" 7 May, 2010.

54 See Howard Zinn, *A People›s History of the United States*, 1980.

55 Ernest E. Judd and Warren, A.P, *Why war is near, conflicting Capitalist interests*, 1931, p. 6.

56 Gabriel Kolko, *The Politics of War*, 1990, p. 251.

57 See Louis Turner, "The Seven Sisters," 1976 (a study of the international oil industry).

58 Howard Zinn, *A People›s History of the United States*, 1980, p. 414.

59 Sam Harris, *The End of Faith*, 2004, p. 65.

60 Ibid., p. 79.

61 Ibid., p. 93.

62 Ibid., p. 108.

63 Ibid., p. 94-96.

64 Ibid., p. 97, 100-104.

65 Even though it is generally agreed the Nazi party was primarily secularly motivated, there is evidence that some of the top Nazi members adopted ancient Sanskrit ideals for their own militant racially driven aspirations. For instance, the bent cross known as the swastika so widely identified with the Nazi party is a sacred symbol of Jainism, Buddhism, and Hinduism. The word Aryan, now forever associated with the Nazi socialist movement, comes from the Sanskrit word "Arya," which means a supreme or pure class. Heinrich Himmler, head of the Nazis' secret

service, "identified himself and the SS with the old Indian Kshatriya caste and its publicized attitude of unscrupulous killing for one's 'higher purpose.'"See Mathias Tietke, Yoga im Nationalsozialismus, 2011, and Yoga in Der DDR: Geächtet, Geduldet, Gefördert, 2014.

66 Ibid.

67 Ibid., p. 148.

68 See Sahih al-Bukhari 2:23:446 and 7:71:670, and Jafar al-Sadiq.

69 See BBC Staff, *Muslims in Burma's Rakhine state "abused" - Amnesty.* BBC News, 20 Jul. 2012.

70 See PEW Staff, *Muslim Publics Share Concerns about Extremist Groups.* Pew Research Center (PEW), 10 Sep. 2013.

71 See Harris/Aslan C-SPAN debate, 20 Jan. 2007.

72 Sam Harris, *End of Faith,* pp. 109-110.

73 For a comprehensive argument that jihad is primarily a defensive theory — including defense of others who cannot defend themselves — and not an offensive theory,See Niaz A. Shah, "The Use of Force under Islamic Law," pgs. 343-365, 1 April 2013.See also Wahebeh Al-Zuhili, *Islam and International Law,* 87 (858), Jun. 2005.

74 Sam Harris, *End of Faith,* p. 110.

75 For definitions and details on certain religious and/or spiritual terms,See Robert Emeritus, and Gregory Alles, *The Encyclopedia of World Religions,* 2007.

76 See Joel Hayward, *Warfare in the Qur'an,* 2012.

77 Sam Harris, *End of Faith,* p. 179.

78 Ibid., p. 192.

79 Ibid., p. 199.

80 Ibid., p. 208.

81 Ibid., p. 212, 221.

82 Ibid., p. 215.

83 Ibid., p. 221.

84 See Dawkins, Richard, *The God Delusion*, 2006.

85 Ronald W Clark, *Einstein: The Life and Times,* 1971, p. 425.

86 Ronald W Clark, *Einstein: The Life and Times,* 1971.

87 William B. Ashworth, Jr., "Scientist of the day - Albert Einstein," Linda Hall Library, 18 Apr. 2023.

88 This is the famous interpretation, but the quote is also oftenSeen as "I, at any rate, am convinced that He is not playing at dice," from his letter to Max Born. Musser, George, "What Einstein Really Thought about Quantum Mechanics," *Scientific American*, 1 Sep. 2015.

89 See G. S. Viereck, G.S., *Glimpses of the Great,* 1930.

90 See Baruch Spinoza, *The Ethics*, 1677. William White Translation, 1883.

91 Dialogue with Einstein, Albert, Murphy James, and Sullivan J.W.N., *Science and God*: Forum and Century 83, June, 1930.

92 Richard Dawkins, *The God Delusion*, 2006, p. 134.

93 Michael Shermer, "Science, Religion and the Meaning of Life," 2015.

94 Ptolemy Tompkins, *Proof of God*, 2017, p. 14.

95 Richard Dawkins, *The God Delusion*. 2006, p. 142.

96 Ibid. p. 147.

97 See Charles Darwin, *On the Origin of Species,* 1859.

98 Isaac Chotiner, "Interview: Richard Dawkins Keeps Making New Enemies," 28 Oct. 2013.

99 Daniel Dennett III, *Darwin's Dangerous Ideas*, 1996, p. 18.

100 Ibid. p. 42.

101 Ibid., p. 60.

102 Ibid. p. 82.

103 Ibid. p. 184.

104 Ibid. p. 518.

105 Ibid. p. 510.

106 Nicomachean Ethics.See H. Rackman, *Aristotle in 23 Volumes*, 1934.

107 Robert Pirsig, *Lila: An Inquiry into Morals*, 1992, pp. 184-185.

108 Daniel Dennett III, *Darwin's Dangerous Ideas*, 1996, p. 185.

109 Huston Smith, *The World's Religions,* 1991, p. 13.

110 Ibid., p. 14.

111 Ibid., p. 14.

112 Ibid., p. 18.

113 Ibid., p. 19.

114 Ibid., p. 21.

115 Ibid., p. 22.

116 Ibid., p. 88.

117 Ibid.

118 See Alan Watts, "The Nature of Consciousness," 1969. Accessed 24 Jun. 2023.

119 See Alan Watts, "Eco Zen" *YouTube*, 2023. Accessed 23 Jun. 2023.

120 Don Lincoln, "The Good Vibrations of Quantum Field Theories," PBS, 5 Aug. 2013

121 Jim Lucas, "What are gamma rays?", Live Science, 29 Nov. 2018.

122 Jim Lucas, "What is visible light?" Live Science, 23 May 2022.

123

Matt Williams, "What is the Big Bang Theory?", Phys.org, 18 Dec. 2015.

124 Fraser Cain, "When was the first light in the universe?", Phys.org, 7 Nov. 2016.

125 Richard McCray, "7. Evolution of the Milky Way," Jila.colorado.edu, 3 March 2002.

126 "Dark Energy, Dark Matter," NASA Science, Accessed 18 Sep. 2023.

127 Ibid.

128 Anthony L. Peratt, "Electric space: Evolution of the plasma universe," Astrophysics and Space Science, March 1996, Volume 244, Issue 1-2, pp. 89-103.

129 See Pallab Ghosh, *Earliest evidence of life on earth found*, BBC News Science, March 1, 2017.

130 Beth Blaxland & Fran Dorey, "Larger brains," Australian Museum, 2 Nov. 2018.

131 Brian Handwerk, *An evolutionary timeline of homo sapiens*, Smithsonian Magazine, February 2, 2021.

132 Klee Irwin, *The Code Theoretic Axiom: The Third Ontology*, Oct. 24, 2017.

133 Ibid.

134 For more information on Werner Heisenberg's theory,See Caltech Faculty, "What Is the Uncertainty Principle and Why Is It Important?", Accessed 18 Sep. 2023.

135 Kate Becker, "Is Information Fundamental?", 2014.

136 Jonathan Westphal, "Descartes and the Discovery of the Mind-Body Problem," The MIT Press Reader, 8 Aug. 2019.

137 See «Purpose and the Universe by Sean M. Carroll,» *YouTube*, 8 Jun. 2013.

138 Edward Kessler, *What Do Jews Believe? The Customs and Culture of Modern Judaism*, 2007, pp. 42-44.

139 Ice core samples taken recently from Kilimanjaro show episodic periods of significant drought throughout Africa starting around 2000 BCE through 1700 BCE (see LG Thompson et al, 2002). Archaeological excavations in modern-day Tell ad-Daba, Egypt, reveal

Semitic settlements (some suggest of Joseph himself) of the same time period which were later abandoned (see Bar-Ron, 2017).

140 See Michael Bar-Ron, "The Seal of Joseph." *Beth Midrash Ohel Moshe*, 29 Dec. 2017.

141 Benedictus de Spinoza, *Tractatus Theologico-politicus*, translated by Robert Willis, 1868.

142 See Finkelstein and Silberman, *The Bible Unearthed*, 2001.

143 In Deuteronomy 18:15 and 18 God promises Moses that he will send a prophet among your midst from your brethren and that he would be like Moses. And God will put his words in this prophet's mouth and he shall speak to the people as God commands.

144 See Exodus 28-1, and Genesis 34 and 49:5-7.

145 See Tom Harpur, *Recovering the Lost Light, The Pagan Christ*, 2004.

146 See Jennifer Michael Hecht, *Doubt: A History*, 2004.

147 See John Walker, *Did a Historical Jesus Exist?*, 1997.

148 See Eric Eve, *Behind the Gospels*, 2014.

149 See Richard Bauckham, *"Jesus and the Eyewitnesses,"* 2006.

150 See Horsley, Richard A., and Draper, Jonathan, *Whoever Hears You Hears Me: Prophets, Performance and Tradition in Q*, Trinity Press, 1999

151 See Luke 1:1-4.

152 See 2 Corinthians 3:12-18.

153 See Elaine Pagels & Karen L. King, *Reading Judas: The Gospel of Judas and the Shaping of Christianity*, 2007.

154 David Ian Miller, "FINDING MY RELIGION / Religious scholar Elaine Pagels on how the newly discovered Gospel of Judas sheds new light on the dawn of Christianity," 2 Apr. 2007.

155 An alleged copy of the Gospel of Barnabas written in Aramaic recently surfaced – confiscated by Turkish officials from a ring of antiquity smugglers – that is said to be over 1500 years old.

156 Qur'an, 4:157-158.

157 See Reza Aslan, *Zealot,* 2014.

158 See Joe Fassler, "The Book That Changed Reza Aslan's Mind About Jesus," *The Atlantic*, 6 Aug. 2013.

159 See Daniel Henson, "Dossier of Reason." Accessed 10 Jan. 2022.

160 The Shia came to believe only a bloodline of the Prophet should assume the religious mantle of caliph or imam. A few months before his passing the Prophet ordered the Muslims to agree to allegiance to Ali. According to a supported Sunni hadith, Muhammad said, "Of whomsoever I am the mawla, Ali is his mawla" (al-Tirmidhi, 3713; Ibn Maajah, 121). Mawla can be used to refer to a friend, a protector or even sometimes as master. Herein the firstSeeds of dispute began between Sunni and Shia Muslims.

161 Alexander Stille, "Scholars Are Quietly Offering New Theories of the Koran," 2 Mar. 2022.

162 Ibid.

163 Sadeghi & Goudarzi, *Sana 1 and the Origins of the Qur›an*, 2012, 87 (1–2): 1–129.

164 See Abul Taher, "Querying the Koran," 8 Aug. 2000.

165 Sadeghi & Bergmann, "The Codex of a Companion of the Prophet and the Qurān of the Prophet," 2010, p. 348.

166 Sean Coughlan, "Oldest Koran Fragments Found in Birmingham University," 22 July 2015.

167 Cadbury Research Library, "Birmingham Qur›an manuscript dated among the oldest in the world," University of Birmingham Press Office, 22 Jul. 2015.

168 Alexander Stille, *Scholars Are Quietly Offering New Theories of the Koran*, 2002.

169 Ibid.

170 Mohammed Arkoun, *Lectures du Coran*, Maisonneuve et Larose 1982.

171 Shankar Sharan, "Fifty Different Tellings of the Quran," 2015.

172 Shias accept some of the Sunni hadith but reject many more, particularly those of Aisha and Abu Hurayrah (of whom 5000 hadith are attributed in approximately a four-year span, or on average about three events a day for four consecutive years). Shias have a number of additional hadith, particularly by Ali of which they give special emphasis.

173 Tariq Ramadan, *Radical Reform*, 2008, p. 90.

174 Ibid., p. 91.

175 Ibid., p. 128.

176 Ibid., p. 146.

177 Ibid., p. 152.

178 Jordan, Gary, host. "Apollo 8: Part 1." *Houston We Have a Podcast*, Dec. 21, 2018.

179 See Judges 5:30-31.

180 See Gen 5:27.

181 See Amos 2:9.

182 See "Human Mortality at Extreme Age," Jun. 29, 2018.

183 Hannah Devlin. Hannah Devlin, "Maximum human lifespan could far exceed 115 years - new research," *The Guardian*, June 28, 2017.

184 Hugh Newman, "Top Ten Giant Discoveries in North America," Ancient Origins, 12 Feb. 2022.

185 See Genesis 7:20 and Psalms 104:5-6.

186 See Genesis 7:14.

187 James Trefil, *Evidence for a Flood-Sediment layers suggest that 7,500 years ago Mediterranean water roared into the Black Sea,* April 1, 2000.

188 See Matthew 27:45-53.

189 Genesis 1:20.

190 Genesis 1:24-31.

191 Peggy Townsend, "Did Life Begin ... on Land?" 19 Jul. 2017.

192 Quran, 2:255.

193 ANU Staff, "Earth Was Barren, Mountainless and Almost Entirely under Water 4.4 Billion Years Ago – ANU Study," *Australian National University*, 9 May 2017.

194 Morgan Smith, "Cosmic Oceans: The Primordial Waters of Ancient Creation Myths," 28 Jul. 2019.

195 Irshaad Hussain, "The Water of Creation," 16 Feb. 2013.

196 Ilsedore Cleeves, et al, *The ancient heritage of water ice in the solar system*, 26 Sep 2014: Vol. 345, Issue 6204, pp. 1590-1593.

197 Quranic citations are taken primarily from the Noorudee Durkee, *Sahih International*, and Rashad Khalifa translations as well as to a lesser extent the Arabic Corpus, Marmaduke Pickthall, and Yusuf Ali. (Although the former appear to be more helpful in forming a more common English vernacular translation).

198 Robert Lacey, *Inside the Kingdom: History of Saudi Arabia from 1979 to date,* 2009, pp. 89–90, 352.

199 NASA Staff, "Will the Universe Expand Forever?" 24 Jan. 2014.

200 Q 21:104.

201 Q 71:15-16.

202 NASA Staff, "The Star Splitters: The Mystery of the Missing Mass," *NASA*. Accessed 21 Feb. 2023.

203 *Sunan al-Tirmidhi*, Hadith no. 1513.

204 *Sunan Abu Dawood*, Hadith no. 2205.

205 *Sahih al-Albani*, Al-Silsilah Al-Sahihah, Hadith no. 109; reported by ibn Hibban, Hadith no. 361.

206 Bucaille, once the personal physician to Anwar Sadat, was afforded the rare opportunity to do an autopsy on the mummy Merneptah (whom he came to believe was the pharaoh of the Exodus). He was at first skeptical, then confounded, when he verified the Quran promised that Pharaoh's body after pursuing Moses and drowning would be preserved as a sign for those who came after him (see Q 10:92). Today the mummified bodies of both Ramses II and Merneptah, having lied buried and entombed lost for centuries, were only recently exhumed and are now lying in the Royal Mummies Hall at the National Museum of Egyptian Civilization on full display for all toSee.

207 Translation by Nanikram Vasanmal Thadani, as quoted in Muhammad Iqbal, *The Reconstruction of Religious Thought in Islam*, 2011, p. 147.

208 See Q 2:30-31. It is commonly understood that what was taught was the name of all objects (such as birds, trees, rocks, etc.) but if so, it would have been quite an exhaustive list. It may also be simply referring to the names of God. Just as the angels had been glorifying God with those praises (special names and attributes) He may have not yet revealed the additional names that He then taught Adam. It is instructive to show that things are taught and revealed in stages. It can thus beSeen as symbolic, not only of the advanced language skills Adam had acquired, but also the spiritual revelations he was given to temper his willful, baser nature.

209 See Joseph Islam article: *Adam (pbuh) an Earthly Abode or Paradise?* 2010.

210 John William Draper, *History of conflict between religion and science*, 1874, p. 188.

211 Leroyce Miles, *Introduction to the Study of Religion*, 2018 pp. 223-225

212 Muhammad Hamidullah and Afzal Iqbal, *The Emergence of Islam: Lectures on the Development of Islamic World-view, Intellectual Tradition and Polity*, 1993, pp. 143-144.

213 Muhammad Sultan Shah, *Pre-Darwinian Muslim Scholars' Views on Evolution,* p. 15.

214 Farid Alakbarli, *A 13th-Century Darwin?* 2001, pp. 48-49.

215 Ibn Khaldun, *The Muqaddimah, An Introduction to History*, 2005, p. 75.

216 Jinn are believed to have the power of flight and the ability to shape shift and disappear into thin air, not unlike reports by some of

Seeing ghosts, apparitions or even aliens. Some such as Jay Alfred and Dr. Ibrahim B. Syed believe they may be plasma life forms. Particles in plasma, through electromagnetic forces can change sizes and have the ability to pass through otherwise solid objects. New studies are revealing under the right conditions (abundant in space), plasmas can form plasma crystals that in turn can form into various configurations (including the double helix found in DNA), and can even reproduce and evolve.

217 See Jay Alfred, "Jinns: Plasma Aliens from a Parallel Planet," 2008. Accessed Jul. 20, 2023.

218 Harun Yahya is the pen name of Adnan Oktar, who was recently convicted of various crimes in Türkiye, and sentenced to 8,568 years in prison. His creationist writings, which are widely available and commented upon, are included to give context to those who agree and disagree with his evolutionary views.

219 Harun Yahya, *Tell me about the creation*, 2002, p. 5.

220 Robert Roy Britt, "Unlikely Cousins: Whales and Hippos," Live Science, 25 Jan. 2004.

221 Harun Yahya, *Tell me about the creation*, 2002, p. 14.

222 Ha Nun Mim Keller, *Islam and Evolution*, 1996.

223 Harun Yahya, *Tell me about the creation*, 2002, p. 60.

224 David Solomon Jalajel, *Islam and Biological Evolution*, 2009, p. 163.

225 Ibid.

226 Evelyn Fox Keller, "A Clash of Two Cultures," 2002.

227 Mike Mcrae, *Scientists Just Found a Vital Missing Link in The Origins of Life on Earth*, 7 Nov. 2017.

228 Perry Marshall, "If You Can Read This Sentence, I Can Prove God Exists," 26 May 2009.

229 See E. M. Elsheik, E.M. "Evolution physical intelligent guiding principle," *Energ. Ecol. Environ.* 1, pp. 75–85, 2016.

230 Ibrahim Kalin, "Sadr al-Din Shirazi (Mulla Sadra) (b. 1571-1640)," Resources on Islam & Science, March 2001.

231 See John Cooper, "Mulla Sadra," 1998.

232 Armstrong, Karen, *The Case for God*, 2009, pp. x-xii.

233 Ratner Joseph, *George Santayana's Theory of Religion*, Vol. 3, No. 5, Sep., 1923, p. 459.

234 Robert Pirsig, *Zen and the Art of Motorcycle Maintenance*, 1974. p. 170.

235 "Keats' Letters," *British Literature Wiki.*

236 John Archibald Wheeler, "Information, physics, quantum: the search for links," 1989.

237 C.S. Lewis, *Mere Christianity*, 1952, p. 21.

238 Francis Collins, *The Language of God*, 2006, p. 164-165.

239 Ibid.

240 S.J. Gould, *Impeaching a self appointed judge*, 1992, pp. 118-121.

241 Francis Collins, *The Language of God*, 2006, p. 139.

242 Ibid. p. 140.

243 Ibid. p. 140-141.

244 Ibid. p. 200.

245 Ibid. p. 205.

246 Ibid. p. 219.

247 Ibid. p. 219.

248 C.S. Lewis, *Mere Christianity*, 1952, p. 21.

249 Ibid. p. 53.

250 C.S. Lewis, *Miracles a preliminary study*, 1960.

251 Klee Irwin, *The Code Theoretic Axiom: The Third Ontology*, Oct. 24, 2017.

252 Ibid.

253 Christopher Langan, "The Cognitive-Theoretic Model of the Universe: A New Kind of Reality Theory," 2002.

254 Ibid·

255 Ibid·

256 Ibid·

257 George Cunningham, *Decoding the Language of God*, 2010, p. 80.

258 Ibid. p. 197.

259 Ibid. p. 180.

260 Ibid. p. 185.

261 Ibid. p. 240.

262 Ibid. p. 244.

263 Tara MacIsaac, "Astronomer Says Spiritual Phenomena Exist in Other Dimensions,"
7 April 2014.

264 Walter Isaacson, *Einstein: His Life and Universe*, 2017, p. 390.

265 See "Bertrand Russell," uploaded by BBC Face to Face, 13 Nov. 1988.

266 See Ibn Al-Haytham, *Al-Shukūk 'alā Batlamyūs (Doubts Concerning Ptolemy)*, 1028.

About the Author

Brandon Mayfield is a practicing attorney in Portland, Oregon. He is an experienced writer and lecturer on various topics, including Islam, civil rights, and forensic science, and has appeared on numerous national news organizations, including Fox News, MSNBC, Al Jazeera, and the BBC. He is the co-author of *Improbable Cause: The War on Terror's Assault on our Civil Rights.* He currently lives in the Greater Portland Area with his wife Mona and 15-year-old daughter, Sumaya, and still enjoys new places to explore and people to meet in the Pacific Northwest.

Other Titles by Crescent Books

The Spectacular Escape by Burhan al-Din Fili, 2023

Kosovo: A Brief Chronology by Flamur Vehapi, 2023

Verses of the Heart: Poems by Flamur Vehapi, 2021

Ertugrul Ghazi: A Very Short Biography by Flamur Vehapi, 2021

Made in the USA
Columbia, SC
27 May 2025

58518768R00126